Items should be returned on or before the last date
shown below. Items not already requested by other
borrowers may be renewed in person, in writing or by
telephone. To renew, please quote the number on the
barcode label. To renew online a PIN is required.
This can be requested at your local library.
Renew online @ **www.dublincitypubliclibraries.ie**
Fines charged for overdue items will include postage
incurred in recovery. Damage to or loss of items will
be charged to the borrower.

**Leabharlanna Poiblí Chathair Bhaile Átha Cliath
Dublin City Public Libraries**

Baile Átha Cliath
Dublin City

Leabharlann na Cabraí
Cabra Library
Tel: 8691414

2016

Date Due	Date Due	Date Due

D1349849

This Place Speaks to Me

This Place Speaks to Me

*An anthology of
people and places by*

JOHN QUINN

VERITAS

Dedication

For George Cunningham, friend, mentor
and passionate lover of place.

Special thanks to my typist, Máire Ní Fhrighil,
for her courage in the face of adversity.

Published 2016 by Veritas Publications
7–8 Lower Abbey Street
Dublin 1, Ireland
publications@veritas.ie
www.veritas.ie

ISBN 978 1 84730 747 7

Cover designed by Lir Mac Cárthaigh, Veritas Publications
Printed in the Republic of Ireland by Watermans Printers Ltd,
Cork

*Veritas books are printed on paper made from the wood pulp of managed
forests. For every tree felled, at least one tree is planted, thereby renewing
natural resources.*

Contents

Foreword

I heard the sounds from outside the window at the top of my grandmother's house.

The aural theatre of my childhood and youth ebbing and flowing from the early crowing morning until the pubs closed, and the Morris Minors and the donkey carts started up for the well-filled journeys home.

The mart was the best sound of all.

Worn-out heavy wood buckled on iron as the carts of *banbhs*, potatoes, fowl and turf circled into town and came to a stop on ditch, road and pathway. Cattle came to town like traffic. Their hooves sloshing and knocking on newly browned gravel, while their bony leathery rumps moved in slow waltz time around the village houses and walls. A new barn and a new brier for the day.

Coughing, throating, phlegming and mooing farming men stood in circles, around corners, in large and small groups in front of or in-between their stock, or they loped sideways and alone on leaning elbows, outside pubs with stubs of Sweet Afton cigarettes stuck onto their lower lips.

High-pitched travelling women at the top of the town begged and sang songs of loss – twenty verses long – shouted orders at children and always finished with a begging refrain.

I listened from the big bed in the front bedroom to the slurping of porter on the street, the beat of the sticks against walls and animals, the pulling of rope against wool and hide, and the farmers' throaty and growled bargaining.

Their tone was low when the deal was being done, but it ended in a higher pitch and with a slap on heavy thighs and satisfied roars, the knuckled and working hands clasped and clapped when the money finally changed hands.

Animal snouts were wide and wet and washy against the walls of our houses. Percussive hooves made music on the loose stones against the muffled and softer turn of ropes and meal and flour bags. And in the swallowed wind of the distance, the laughter of deals and night-time delights could be heard.

At Mass on Mart Sunday we would answer the priest like trained chanters, finding our own pitch-perfect refrain, swaying in tweedy voice and inflection as though in a trance. A ritual of sound echoed weekly at Amen funerals or at the Corpus Christi procession when 'Sweet Heart of Jesus' became disconnected as it wafted through the long town in the air and in the echo. Neither the words nor the melody ever met again until the following year.

Aural sound and sound sense were born for me on those musky eiderdown days, behind the top window of my grandmother's house on main street. Aural sound was to be my first introduction to theatre, to the arts and to the unbounding possibilities of radio and writing and teaching. It was my beginning and my understating of how my place spoke to me. It spoke to me through the music and melody and patterns and inflections and phraseology and emphasis and pitch and lift and fall of the word music of the human voice.

It is my sound memory that has held onto every memory of my past. It is the one I carry with me everywhere. My first 'on the ear' experiences. And it has fuelled and fired and given voice to all that I have attempted across the arts and teaching and politics.

I have never left that bedroom.

I have never left that life sound drama.

The places may have changed, but the word music of those young aural days continues. I am just an aural story traveller. A sound companion to myself and others.

That window in County Mayo placed, enmeshed, intertwined and forged me, becoming my launching pad across all times, boundaries and ageing limitations. It was to be my touchstone and my code sign all my life.

This Place Speaks to Me is just such a story book. It is about how we can return and give memory to our own walk, our own memory, our own influence, our own heartbeat, and our own human foundation. In our own way.

Its author, John Quinn, has given each writer, poet, historian, sculptor, artist, thinker and traveller, including me, what Seamus Heaney called 'room to rhyme'.

From Skellig Rock to Ballyfin, from Tyrone to Westmeath and on to Galway and Monaghan, from Jerusalem and Wicklow to Warsaw and Tara, and from Ephesus to Anahorish Primary School, across and around our island north and south, and beyond, the stories of binding places and people and their profound and lasting influence on all the writers, seep through.

This book is about how those life landscapes, places and people moulded the immediate and the far-off memory of the storytellers, and became, for them all, fundamental to their character and perception.

These are their heart hills, their drumlins, their valleys, their hedges and fields, their historic chord monuments, their sanctities, their tribes, known and unknown, renowned and secret. These are the worlds that ignited and indeed kindled something in their imagination, creativity and learning, and held it there in their heads and in their senses forever. Just as my journey of sound, human and natural, did for me.

My aural memory is my memory echo, my tune. It is my story living on my lips, forever. It may even be something akin to the Sweet Afton cigarette held tight on the lips of the County Mayo farmer, still in my memory standing astride the snug, perceptive and silent, with little to say but with a world echoing through his pull, drag and blow as he watched his world reveal itself. He left all the talking and the writing up to others.

I thank the wireless man John Quinn for giving me the opportunity to write a foreword to such a journey of authenticity for all the contributors. And to have had the privilege of being the first to be around their journeys. They are yours – the readers – now.

I thank John Quinn also for reminding us all about our need to be connected to place and the part that such connections play in our lives as we grow and age.

And, most especially, I thank him for reminding me that without stories, especially the ones that formed us when we didn't know it was happening, we would not be able to hang on to what is best about us, and within us, and what really makes our hearts beat passionately.

Marie-Louise O'Donnell
July 2016

Introduction

I have always been intrigued by the power of place to influence our lives – how a landscape, its people and its story can affect our perspective and worldview. During my time as a radio producer I made two series of programmes entitled *This Place Speaks to Me*, which sought to explore that influence. In each case, I invited a guest to pore over their formative years of childhood, or an adopted home in later life or indeed a lifelong residency. This book contains a selection from these programmes, plus a number of locations I have been privileged to visit in a personal capacity over the years.

The resulting stories do not always carry a positive imprint. There are stories of suffering, of deprivation, of evil from prison, from battlefields, from a concentration camp. To balance that, there are stories of sacred spaces which inspire peace and devotion, of landscapes and locations – rural and urban – which profoundly influenced writers and artists. In some instances, individuals – be it a schoolmaster, a librarian, a lady of the manor – have left their mark on a place. In others it is simply the place and its story – be it a midlands bog, a bustling city, a big house, a seaside town or an ancient monastic site – that leaves its imprint. In each case my hope is that the chosen sites in this collection speak eloquently and with insight to all who would listen.

John Quinn
March 2016

Seamus Heaney

on Anahorish Primary School

This is a journey of the mind. The school is long gone and Seamus and I never got any further than his attic study in Dublin. His memories of the time and the place, however, ring out as clearly as Master Murphy's tuning fork 'when he took us for singing lessons, but couldn't sing himself ...'

Anahorish Primary School, which I attended in the late 1940s, no longer stands.

> My 'place of clear water',
> the first hill in the world
> where springs washed into
> the shiny grass
>
> and darkened cobbles
> in the bed of the lane.
>
> ('Anahorish')

The school has very clear memories for me, however, none clearer that those of my very first day there. I was disconsolate, weeping, didn't want to go. Being the eldest of the family, I was the first to go to school and my father, adopting a stern *paterfamilias* role, scolded me, telling me

I had to go and that was that. I can empathise with 'Wee Hughie' of that song that was so popular.

> He's gone to school, Wee Hughie
> And him not four…

I would have been 'not five' when I set off for Anahorish, taken in hand by a neighbour's child, Phil McNicholl. I was put in the care of Miss Walls in the infants' classroom. There had been compensation offered in the form of a new schoolbag, made by a local cobbler.

> … I shouldered it, half-full of blue-lined jotters,
> And saw the classroom charts, the displayed bean,
>
> The wall-map with its spray of shipping lanes
> Describing arcs across the blue North Channel.
> And in the middle of the road to school
> Ox-eye daisies and wild dandelions.
>
> ('The Schoolbag')

Miss Walls was a kindly surrogate mother figure. I remember particularly her telling us fairytales and initiating us into the mysteries of life.

> Miss Walls would tell us how
> The daddy frog was called a bullfrog
> And how he croaked and how the mammy frog
> Laid hundreds of little eggs and this was
> Frogspawn.
>
> ('Death of a Naturalist')

Here with Miss Walls, beginning with slates, we learned the
joy of writing.

> There he draws smoke with chalk the whole first week
> Then draws the forked stick that they call a Y,
> This is writing, A swan's neck and a swan's back
> Make the 2 he can now see as well as say.
>
> Two rafters and a cross-tie on the slate
> Are the letter some call ah, some call ay.
> There are charts, there are headlines, there is a right
> Way to hold the pen and a wrong way.
>
> First it is 'copying out' and then 'English'
> Marked correct with a little leaning hoe.
> Smells of inkwells rise in the classroom hush.
> A globe in the window tilts like a coloured O.
>
> ('Alphabets')

We progressed to headlines transcribed from the board or
from Vere Foster copybooks –

> Time and tide wait for no man.

I remember with affection the lines on those copybooks –
pink and light duck-egg blue. I came across one the other
day and it went straight to the heart. One of the great joys
then was getting a new copybook – and hoping you wouldn't
blot it!

Soon – about Second Class, I suppose, we moved up to 'The Master's Room'. The master was Barney Murphy, a very imposing figure who wore a winged collar and a waistcoat and had a slightly mottled face. This was a more sombre place, more like a nineteenth-century world – which was indeed the world he had come from. Master Murphy had quite an abrupt manner – we knew things were in earnest now. He set his standards high, particularly in poetry. We learned great slabs of Byron, Tennyson, Keats. I knew the 'Ode to Autumn' before I was eleven. I remember on my first day in St Columb's College in Derry, when just to settle us in, a teacher asked each new boy to recite a poem. I gave him the 'The Eve of Waterloo':

> There was a sound of revelry by night
> And Belgium's capital had gathered then
> Her beauty and her chivalry, and bright
> The lamps shone o'er fair women and brave men.

It was like learning the Catechism – full of big words we didn't understand – but I still remember those poems and am grateful for learning them.

Our reading material was limited enough. There was a school 'library' – a padlocked box that came from Coleraine and was moved around. I remember reading Maurice Walsh's *Blackcock's Feather* and Stevenson's *Treasure Island*. The first book that I owned was *Kidnapped* – with a coloured picture on the front. There was also a great barter market in comics. One of my great resentments was that I never had the *Beano* or the *Dandy* ordered for me, but I eventually got my mother to place an order for the *Champion*. It was full of stories of heroes like Johnny Redskin, the boy from the Indian Plains who could play football in his bare feet ... We also got *Our Boys*, possibly as a cultural antidote to the other stuff.

I never made the slightest attempt at writing at Anahorish School. I was particularly stilted. We wrote compositions of course but the system demanded that you tried to write like everyone else as much as you could. You told a bundle of lies in writing up the formal thing that everybody said. Similarly with workbook exercises on stuff like similes. 'Complete the following – as brave as ...' The 'correct' answer was 'a lion'. You didn't want to be too original or else you would be 'wrong'! I didn't really realise that you could tell the truth in writing until I was in my twenties – and in a way that's why I started to write.

I suppose I had a fascination with words. I was intrigued by the dial on the wireless that had names like Hilversum, Stuttgart and Leipzig, and I loved listening to the shipping forecast on the BBC. It is an innate thing in childhood to be fascinated by sounds. We would have fun with nonsense rhymes that were very different to the verse Master Murphy taught us.

> One fine October's morning
> September last July
> The moon lay thick upon the ground
> The mud shone in the sky
> I stepped into a tramcar

> To take me across the sea
> I asked the conductor to punch my ticket
> He punched my eye for me
> I fell in love with an Irish girl
> She sang me an Irish dance
> She lived in Tipperary
> Just a few miles out of France.

When I did the eleven plus exam I was too young to go on to secondary school, so I deferred the scholarship for a year. In that extra year, Master Murphy prepared me for second level. I would go into school early for tuition in Latin, Algebra and Irish. He was a real *dominie*, a master who commanded respect. He would witness or sign documents for people. I remember the one-to-one moments when he would bring us up around his desk for reading or grammar exercises, and I loved when he took us (boys only!) outside for gardening.

When I wrote the poem 'Station Island', I devoted a section to a vision of Master Murphy on Lough Derg, when I imagined meeting him on the island on a pilgrimage. I had in mind the marvellous canto in Dante's *Inferno* where he meets his old teacher Brunetto Latini, but Brunetto was what they called a sodomite and so was down in the other place. I thought old Barney deserved purgatorial status at worst.

A Vision of Master Murphy on Lough Derg

> His sockless feet were like the dried broad-bean
> That split its stitches in the display jar

High on a window-ledge in the old classroom.
White as shy faces in the classroom door.
'Master,' those elders whispered, 'I wonder, master...'
Rustling letters, proffering, withdrawing,
And 'Master' I repeated to myself
So that he stopped but did not turn or move,
His shoulders going small and quiet, his head
Vigilant in the cold gusts off the lough.
I moved ahead and faced him, shook his hand:
'Seamus Heaney, master, from Mossbawn.'
Above the winged collar, his mottled face
Went distant in a smile, as the voice
Readied itself and scraped and husked, 'Good man,
Good man, Heaney,' before it lapsed again
In the limbo and dry urn of the larynx.
The Adam's apple in its weathered sac
Worked like the plunger of a pump in drought,
But yielded nothing to help the helpless smile.
Barney Murphy wrought hard in his day.
Not a one of them in the Creagh Meadows
Could hold foot to him when it came to mowing.
He came through everything that they came through,
Politics and funerals and dunghills,
To stand in front of us, their childrens' children,
In his insignia: the silver watch
And watch-chain, the fountain pen and polished shoes.
And girded in them still, he attended.
'You would have thought that Anahorish School
Was purgatory enough for any man,'

I said, seeing a swarm of scholars
Darken the tall-hedged road for fifty years,
Alfie Kirkwood, smelling of eel-oil,
Who wore an eel-skin on his wrist for strength,
Billy Hunter, with turf-mould in his nails,
Martha Clarke, freckled, with ginger hair,
Shy and sharp as a wild thing in the ditch.
Fetor and field-smells came past on the wind.
The sex-cut of sweet briar after rain.
Littered chestnut pith, birds' nests filled with leaves.
Then a little trembling happened and his breath
Rushed the air softly as scythes in his lost meadows.
'Birch trees have overgrown Leitrim moss.
Dairy herds are grazing where the school was
And the school garden's loose black mould is grass –
But you'll remember it, and the silver florin
I gave you for a prize on your last day.'
'Master, God rest and bless you,' I began
And he was gone and I was faced wrong way
Into pilgrims absorbed in this exercise.
As I turned to join their whispers and bare feet
The mists of those lost mornings I set out
For Latin classes with him, face to face,
Refreshed me. *Mensa, mensa, mensam.*
Sang in the air like a busy whetstone.

Eibhlís de Barra
on the Coal Quay, Cork

It is a warm August day in 1998. Storyteller Eibhlís de Barra is taking me around scenes of her Cork childhood. I could listen all day to the music of her accent and the richness of her idiom. We visit the Lough and the Mardyke, but when we come to the Coal Quay, the scene of Cork's open-air market, the place positively sings to Eibhlís and she in turn sings to me.

My gran was the first to bring me down here. My dad had died in his thirties and left Mam a widow with seven children under eleven years. Gran was strict but she never refused us anything. She wouldn't give us sweets but would buy us duck eggs instead for nourishment. She'd take us into town and buy us a glass of hot milk and a bun with no sugar. Sugar was bad for you. She was sensible like that. She had a memory of the famine times that was handed down to her. Her one idea was that every penny should go to putting food on the table – food, food, food.

No day was complete for the women of Cork without going down to the Coal Quay. The morning was the best time to go. At about eleven o'clock the dealers would come and throw down their bundles of old clothes and start selling. There was great fun and banter about the place.

'Look at that lovely jacket, missus. Your husband would be a real Dickie Dasher in that!' My mother was a dressmaker, so she could buy a woman's coat for thruppence, bring it home, turn it inside out and rip it. Then put a bit of velvet on the collar and we'd have a new coat – all handsome on Sunday for thruppence! The best bargain she ever got was from the button-dealer, who had a tea chest full of button samples. There would be a gross (one hundred and forty-four) of buttons on each card, all different colours for tuppence. Mam went searching down through the chest until she found six identical cards, which she bought for a shilling. The six gross of buttons set her up for life. She could put matching buttons on every coat and dress she made for us. And if we lost the markers when playing Ludo, we'd get four little buttons to replace them. We had them for years and years. What a bargain for a shilling!

Just after the war, the bananas came in and we went stone mad for them. We didn't want poppies (potatoes) nor cabbage no more, Mam would have to come down here for a shilling's worth of bananas. The dealers would know she was a widow and they would keep the big ones for her – batons we'd call them – and we'd have them for breakfast, dinner and supper. Of course there was a great vegetable market here too. The market gardeners would be here at dawn from places like Ballyphehane with their horses and butts (carts) full of cabbages, leeks, celery, turnips and, of course, potatoes.

'Look at them, Mam. Balls of temptation!' the potato dealer would call out. And the farmers' wives would have eggs and country butter for selling to the shops. Because those dealers were in town so early, the pubs were allowed open at 7a.m. to let them in for a drink. Kattie Barry had a famous shebeen that opened late at night. She was a great character. Then there were the eating houses where the farmers went for big mugs of tea and 'baats' of bread and maybe a bit of black pudding. Nothing dainty or such. Wasn't it grand for them?

You got your fish here too. They'd be selling outside that white building. Not much hygiene! The fish woman would have an old block of timber for chopping the fish – herrings, mackerel and eels, even. The sprats were very popular. We don't eat them now but the workmen loved them. All you had to do was cut off the head and the little gut came away with it. Boil them with an onion and the little bones would melt, catch them by the tail and throw them back, no problem. My grandfather always said they were the cleanest little fish in the sea. The fish dealers would sell *duileasc* too – the purple seaweed they have up in the north.

Of course Cork was a city of smells then. Yes, the river smelled but you would also get the lovely malty smell from Beamish's and down by Woodford Bourne's, the smell of coffee grinding. There were bakeries all over the place, so you'd have the smell of hand-baked bread. When I started work at age fourteen, I'd be running home for my dinner. Every door would be open, so you'd know who had the cabbage, who had the bodice (cheap pig meat) or the crubeens, or the parsnips. As for the lucky ones who had steak and onions, that smell would fairly fly out the door! I often say I'd nearly prefer to have the smell of the river back and those smells too, because there are no smells at all here now.

Apart from the stalls, there were loads of little shops here in the Coal Quay, selling furniture, books, records, sewing machines – and gramophones. My mother loved the gramophone. She saw a lovely one here once, put a few bob down on it, sent the old one into Barry's Auction Rooms, sold that and bought the new one. It was beautiful. You'd open it up and there were little doors inside and there was a little brush that went ahead of the needle to keep the record clean. But we had to hide it under the bed when Gran visited us. She'd murder us for wasting our money. She was still the head of the clan! When it was playing, someone would have to stand at the head of the street to watch out for Gran! It was a wind-up machine. Mam would warn us only to give it thirteen winds. If you went over that, you could break the spring and then it would be into the pram with it and down to Bachelor's Quay where a man in a little room would fix it for a few pennies. We had a stack of records a couple of feet high. Mam loved John McCormack. She'd buy his records for thruppence each and for us she'd buy Jimmy O'Dea – 'Casey at the Dentist', 'Casey at the Races', 'Casey at the Pawnshop'. We loved them.

Over there at that stone building, all the butchers had their stalls. We used call them 'the randy butchers'. It was nothing to do with their private lives. They would sell you a bit of goat as quick as they'd look at you, pretending it was mutton. The goat is known to be randy – hence 'the randy butchers'. Everything was boiled in those days, because there were no ovens. We ate a lot of pig meat – right down to the crubeens and the tail. A shilling's worth of cheap meat could provide a good dinner.

The Coal Quay was a great place for entertainment too. Wherever there was a crowd, fellows would come doing all kinds of acts. One fellow would turn himself into a monkey, twisting his legs over his arms and making a monkey-shape. Another would lie on a bed of broken glass or nails. And there would be chancers like the fellow who had this magic stain remover. He would call a little boy from the audience, throw ink on his shirt and then rub away the ink with this block of blue stuff. My mother was delighted at this, bought the blue stuff, brought it home and threw ink over my brother's good Communion shirt. She began rubbing it with the 'magic' stuff and of course if she was rubbing it still, it wouldn't work. The shirt was destroyed. 'The devil hoist that fellow,' she cried. 'If I ever see him again, I'll reef him!' And of course she never did see him again.

There would be fights now and then, but they wouldn't beat one another at all. We'd all run to see the fight, but before it really started they would be pulled off each other. It was like *Coronation Street* – all pretend. Banjo Annie would come of a Saturday night and play songs like 'Two Little Girls in Blue'. Another fellow entertained us on a Saturday night with Shakespeare. He'd light candles and perform in one of the stalls. He'd do the Shakespeare all wrong but it was brilliant altogether! Sure where would you get entertainment like that for nothing?

It was all life here in the Coal Quay. To me this was the real heart of old Cork – much more than Patrick Street. I loved coming here.

Yasnaya Polyana

A personal visit to the birthplace and home of the writer
Leo Tolstoy.

Yasnaya Polyana. Say it again. Yasnaya Polyana. There is
music to its sounding. It might well be a place name from a
Russian novel. And of course it is Russian, but not from a
novel. It is the birthplace and home for much of his life of
the great Russian writer Leo Tolstoy. The house and estate
are maintained today as a memorial museum to the great
man, and I have come to visit it on 25 September 2003 with
a group of Irish tourists.

We have made the two-hundred-kilometre trip by coach
from our base in Moscow. On our way we have stopped off
at another literary museum – the home of Anton Chekhov
at Melikovo, where he wrote *Uncle Vanya* and *The Seagull*. It
has been a moving experience to stand in Chekhov's study
by the desk where these works were realised. But an even
deeper experience lies ahead of us as we disembark from
our coach at the entrance gate to Yasnaya Polyana.

We pass through the imposing stone turrets of the
entrance gate and proceed along the avenue lined with silver
birches towering some fifty feet above us. Tolstoy loved
this avenue or *preshpekt* as it is called. Our leader, Colman,
reminds us that it would have featured in Tolstoy's writing,

notably in *War and Peace*, when Prince Andrei rides along the preshpekt on his return to his home in Bald Hills. At last we emerge from the birches to behold Tolstoy's house. It is an impressive two-storey building, painted white, which has been developed from a wing of the original house built by Tolstoy's grandfather early in the nineteenth century.

A tall, severe-looking lady emerges from the house. She is to be our guide. In dress and general appearance she could well pass as a character from a Tolstoy novel. We understand she is actually related to the writer. The entire house and furnishings have been preserved as they would have been in Tolstoy's final years. The entrance hall is lined with book cabinets, part of the huge personal library of twenty-two thousand volumes that Tolstoy amassed over his lifetime. On a crook hangs the mailbag in which letters, newspapers and magazines were brought here daily from the railway station.

The study has been so meticulously preserved that one could imagine that the great man had just stepped out for a walk in the garden to crystallise his thinking on the next episode of *War and Peace*. There is the Persian walnut desk at which most of his great works were written. Pens in a ceramic bowl. Books strewn where he had left them, candles snuffed out on 28 October 1910, when Tolstoy left this house for the last time. What ruminations, what plottings, what imaginings must have taken place in these simple surroundings. We are told that Tolstoy would go for an early morning walk on his beloved estate and then write for four or five hours. He would then give the rough copy with notes and emendations to his wife Sophia who would make a fair copy of the work – 'a difficult job,' she claimed, 'because what I have written today will probably all be crossed out and rewritten by Leo tomorrow.'

This is a big house but generally the rooms are quite small – probably easier to heat in the harsh winters. The largest room is the dining room, which also served as a gathering room for the young people. Leo and Sophia Tolstoy had thirteen children so this room would have been noisy. On top of that, many artists and writers (among them Gorky, Turgenev and Chekhov) came and stayed as guests. The sumptuous meals served at the long dining table would have been occasions for lively conversations and often heated arguments. The longer Tolstoy lived, the more intolerant he became of the affluent lifestyle of houses like Yasnaya Polyana, compared to the poverty of the peasants who lived on his estate.

> More and more, almost physically, I suffer from the disparity: the wealth and the excess of our life in the midst of poverty. And I cannot lessen this disparity. Herein lies the secret tragedy of my life … Masses of people, all of them well-dressed, eat, drink, demand. Servants run back and forth carrying out orders. And I find it more and more distressing and more and more difficult to take part in this without condemning it. We are sitting outside, eating ten different foods and ice-cream, surrounded by footmen and silver, when beggars arrive. And the good people continue calmly eating their ice-creams. Amazing!!!

We pass through Leo and Sophia's bedroom. Simply adorned. Sparsely furnished. In Sophia's room, a writing table where she kept household accounts and wrote letters and diaries. On the wall above her dressing table hang family photographs and her sketches of plants and flowers. She was a busy woman.

Our group moves outside to walk through the woods in search of Tolstoy's grave. It is autumn in Yasnaya Polyana. Already there is a carpet of leaves underfoot – russet and brown and burnt gold. I pick up a few and secrete them in an envelope. They will make attractive bookmarks. We pause at the 'Lover Trees' – two tall trees that have interlaced and enfolded each other like lovers over the years. All is peace and tranquillity. Little wonder that these surroundings inspired and intoxicated Tolstoy.

> That marvellous smell of the woods after a spring thundershower; the odour of birches, violets, mouldy leaves, mushrooms and bird cherry blossoms is so delightful that I cannot sit still in my carriage but jump from the running-board, run over to the bushes and in spite of getting showered with raindrops, tear off wet branches of bird cherry blossoms, beat my face with them and become drunk with their wondrous smell …

Tolstoy liked physical labour and would often join with the peasants on his estate, toiling in the fields both to show solidarity with the peasants and experience 'the most blissful state, the happiest hours in life – the hours of toil in the field'. We pass near another cause dear to Tolstoy – the school that he established for the children of Yasnaya Polyana and where he occasionally taught and told stories:

> When I enter the school and see the crowd of tattered, dirty, skinny children with their bright eyes and so often angelic expressions, I am filled with an alarm and horror like that which I might feel at the sight of drowning people. Ah, saints alive, how can they be pulled out and who should be first and who later? And it is what is most dear that is drowning here, namely that spiritual element which so obviously strikes the eye in children. I want education for the people only in order to save the Pushkins drowning here ...

On 28 October 1910, Leo Tolstoy made a decision. He could no longer live with such disparity in society. He wanted to renounce wealth and possessions but his wife and family would not hear of it. His position in the house had become unbearable. So he would leave Yasnaya Polyana. He wrote a letter to Sophia, packed a few essential things in a bag and slipped away in the night with his secretary Makovitsky to catch a train on which he insisted on travelling third class. His 'escape' was all too brief however. He took ill on the journey, developed pneumonia and was taken to the station master's house at Astapovo where he died on 7 November. Two days later his body returned by train to Yasnaya Polyana where a large assembly of peasants, students and dignitaries waited to pay their last respects.

According to his wishes, Leo Tolstoy was buried in a clearing in the woods of his beloved Yasnaya Polyana. As a child he had heard from his older brother of the legend of a magic green wand. The secret of constant happiness and freedom from any misfortune was written in a green wand that was buried at the roadside. Tolstoy wished to be buried where the green wand lay.

And so we tourists have come to Leo Tolstoy's resting place: a simple raised mound in a clearing under the shade of two giant trees. No marking stone, no ornaments, no flowers, no wreaths. A mound strewn with evergreen branches. A time to be silent, to reflect and pray, to withdraw respectfully.

We make our way back through the woodland and go slowly down the birch-lined avenue. Soon we will leave the peace of the Russian countryside and return to the bustle of Moscow. The words of Leo Tolstoy echo in my mind:

Without my Yasnaya Polyana
I would have a hard time
imagining Russia and my relation to her …

Diarmuid Breathnach
on Bray Promenade

Historian, author and former librarian Diarmuid Breathnach
has lived most of his life in Bray, County Wicklow. In 1998
we took a stroll along the seafront which in Victorian times
was designated 'Ireland's premier seaside resort'.

Our stroll begins on 'Fiddler's Bridge' at the southern end
of the town. It offers what Diarmuid calls a 'preserved view'
of the town. The seafront stretches before us like a view
from a Victorian painting. Diarmuid picks out the details.

'According to the topography expert Liam Price, Bray
gets its name from the river Brí (now the Dargle), which
in turn may have been the name of an ancient goddess.
In the eighteenth century, visitors to Bray were attracted
to the Dargle valley which stretched away west of the
town. The seafront then would not have been the most
salubrious of locations. The town was dominated by a few
large estates. The white house on our left, now the Loreto
convent, was then Sans Souci, the home of the Putland
family. They owned all of this part of Bray right down to
the sea. Behind us on Bray Head is Raheenacluig, the ruin
of an Augustinian oratory, a reminder that these lands once
belonged to the Abbey of St Thomas, but in Tudor times
they were confiscated and given to the Brabazons who

became the Earls of Meath. Further inland the Edwards family had a castle on the Oldcourt Estate. A lot of families who had done the "Grand Tour" in Europe called their homes after places they had visited – Palermo, Vallombrosa, Vevay – but the town itself needed an injection of life in the mid-nineteenth century. And that came with the investment by William Dargan in the revolutionary mode of travel – the railway. Bringing the railway to Bray transformed the town, and in particular opened up the seafront.

'William Dargan was a businessman, a wealthy entrepreneur and a complex character in many ways. He had a great spirit of patriotism which was badly needed in a country recovering from the ravages of the Famine. The railway was already on its way to Bray under the direction of the great engineer Isambard Brunel, but Dargan invested heavily in the railway and in the town. There were five hundred men employed in the building of the railway which would have helped offset the devastation of the Famine. It must have been a source of great pride to Dargan when the Dublin–Bray railway line opened on 10 July 1854. He was the greatest historical figure in the development of Bray. There is no memorial to him here like the statue outside the National Gallery in Dublin, to which he made a huge contribution – but I suppose the railway station is his monument. He gave much more to Bray, as we'll see when we go "promenading" …'

On our way down to the Promenade we pass by 'the Cove', which was a very popular swimming area in the first half of the twentieth century. There is a wonderful painting by Harry Kernoff that shows how truly popular the Cove was. Nearby, a cable car ran up Bray Head to 'Eagle's Nest', a dance hall-cum-restaurant. It was a great attraction until tourism declined when the car ferries opened up the possibility of holidays abroad.

'The railway created Bray as a seaside resort. The town was marketed as "the Brighton of Ireland – Ireland's premier seaside resort". To achieve that, the seafront was transformed. Dargan created the esplanade – a huge green garden area that ran the length of the front. Later came the promenade where we are strolling now – a magnificent mile-long walkway between the esplanade and the sea. People went strolling to see and be seen. It was a big social occasion – you might meet someone you know and walk with them in another direction. I remember my mother would come down here when a mystery tour came to the town – in the hope that she might meet someone from Tipperary! The Victorians experienced "hydromania" – a madness for water. They wanted to breathe the sea air and watch the wildness of the sea. Bathing was not a priority – the restrictions on mixed bathing were quite severe. Dargan even built a Turkish Baths on Quinsboro Road. The Victorians didn't necessarily come for the sunshine either. If you look at old photographs, you will see a lot of large black parasols. It wasn't fashionable to have a tan – the Victorians preferred to be "pale and interesting"!

'As the seafront developed, many wealthy families built houses either as holiday homes or as investment properties – families such as the Guinnesses, the Elverys and the

Wildes. What is now Kinvara House Nursing Home was a series of houses built by Sir William Wilde, father of Oscar, to provide him with a pension in later life. The same Sir William, a famous surgeon, was the focus of a major scandal. A Miss Travers alleged that he had interfered with her and published her story in a pamphlet which was sold around the town. Lady Wilde wrote a letter to Miss Travers' father, which became the subject of a libel case. Ultimately Miss Travers won a farthing damages – which meant in reality that she lost ...'

As we approach the northern end of the Promenade we face an imposing terrace of houses – Martello Terrace, under the shadow of a Martello tower ('where Bono once lived', Diarmuid reminds me). A plaque on the wall informs me that 'James Joyce, poet and novelist, lived here 1887–91'.

'James would have been five then. His father was a well-off man who owned several properties in Cork. When they moved here, it would have been a lovely, healthy place to live, with an unbroken view of Bray Head. Joyce immortalised the dining room here when he wrote the Christmas dinner scene in *A Portrait of the Artist as a Young Man*, involving a huge row about Parnell and the Church's treatment of him. Present were Joyce's parents (Mr and Mrs Dedalus in the book), Mrs Conway (Dante), John Kelly (Mr Casey) and Uncle Charles ...'

Today, No. 1 is the home of politician Liz McManus and her husband John. She graciously invites us into the famous dining room that still speaks to her ... 'I'm always conscious of another little boy growing up with my own boys here.

The Christmas dinner was a very typical family scene where people say the wrong things and fireworks ensue!' We happen to have a couple of copies of *A Portrait* with us and an impromptu reading of the dinner scene ensues … It is hot and heavy stuff with Mr Dedalus pouring scorn on the bishops – 'Billy with the lip … and tub of guts up in Armagh'. Dante defends them, claiming 'there could be neither luck nor grace in a house where there is no respect for the pastors of the Church'. Mr Dedalus will have none of it, denouncing the priests who turned on Parnell when he was down – 'to betray him and rend him like rats in a sewer …'

We cross the railway track. Across from the station are the Carlisle Grounds, today home of Bray Wanderers Football Club. Diarmuid relates its origins.

'This is another example of Dargan's development of Bray. There had been athletic meetings on the esplanade but too many of the common people were intruding, so Dargan marked out a large area here as a sports ground for the wealthier classes. It was opened in 1862 by the Lord Lieutenant, the Earl of Carlisle – hence the name. It was originally the cricket, croquet and archery grounds, but all sorts of sports were featured – polo, lawn tennis, even skating with demonstrations by Russian skaters. There were balloon ascents, agricultural and flower shows. Everything that was new in entertainment came to Bray, and Dargan was the prime mover. He built the huge International Hotel across the road. It was destroyed by fire in the 1960s. He opened up the town to the sea by building Quinsboro Road, which we are standing on. It was known as the Forty Foot Road, simply because it was forty feet wide. This town owes him so much, even though as an entrepreneur he lost money here. Over a century later, Dargan's stamp is very much on the town of Bray, particularly the seafront area.'

I part with Diarmuid and enter the railway station to catch a modern DART back to Dublin. It is a busy place, but amid the hum and clack of DART trains, I have only to close my eyes and imagine another era of steam and smoke, when sixty trains a day would depart for either Harcourt Street or Westland Row in the city. And there, amid the clouds of steam, I fancy I see a well-suited businessman consulting his pocket watch as another train disgorges its passengers who have come to experience the 'Brighton of Ireland' ...

Douglas Gageby
on Belfast

Although born in Dublin, Douglas Gageby, former editor of *The Irish Times*, spent his childhood and schooldays in the northern city. In 1998, just months after the Good Friday Agreement brought peace to Northern Ireland, Douglas and I revisited significant locations in the Belfast of his youth.

We begin on Cave Hill, overlooking the city, famous in political history and above all noted as the playground for people living in the north of Belfast. For about twenty years I lived in Belfast and I would be all around this place with my pals every week. Above us is the imposing Mac Art's Fort – a basalt rock jutting out over the city. I often stood there on a summer evening and watched four boats sailing out beneath me in Belfast Lough to Liverpool, Glasgow, Heysham and Ardrossan. They looked like little toys with cotton wool smoke rising from their chimneys, from my vantage point eleven hundred feet above. Below was all the beauty of Belfast Lough and all the clamour of the shipyards, the trams and the factory hooters. I remember getting the fright of my life late one summer evening, standing at the edge of a steep, precipitous cliff, when suddenly a big white face appeared silently in front of me. I looked at it, it looked at me and then dropped down. It was the first time I saw a barn owl.

But these were the carefree days of boyhood when I explored that lovely place, picked bilberries or fried eggs and bacon in a billycan over a little fire. This place was aptly named Bellevue. Then it had a dancehall, a clock-golf-course and cafeterias. There would be concert parties given by little travelling vaudevillian groups, gathered at the bandstand.

Alice Milligan captures this place so well in her poem, 'Ben Madigan':

> Look up from the streets of the city,
> Look high beyond tower and mast,
> What hand and what type of sculptor
> Smote the crags on the mountain vast?
> Made when the world was fashioned,
> Meant with the world to last,
> The glorious face of the sleeper
> That slumbers above Belfast.

My friend Paddy Scott says that Padraig Pearse once called this place 'Ireland's holy mountain', referring to the famous day in June 1795 when Wolfe Tone wrote in his diary:

> I remember two days we spent on the Cave Hill. On the first Russell, Neilson, Simms, McCracken and one or two more of us on the summit of Mac Art's Fort took a solemn obligation which I think I may say I have on my part endeavoured to fulfil – never to desist in our

efforts until we had subverted the authority of England over our country and asserted our independence.

After the Troubles of the past thirty years and previous to that, there is the hope that we are moving into a new dispensation with the new administration. Pray for Belfast! I remember during the power-sharing executive, one member of the SDLP said to me, 'Wee Brian's [Faulkner] all right to work with. He has his wild men behind him. We understand that.' Similarly I would hear from the Unionist side: 'These boys are okay. We can work with them.' We hear a lot about a pan-Nationalist front, but we hear little about a pan-Christian front. Away back in the eighties a Presbyterian minister, the Rev. Robin Boyd, gave the 'Thought for the Day' on RTÉ Radio. We reprinted his words on *The Irish Times* front page the following day. Rev. Boyd was talking about the Presbyterian dilemma, although it applies equally to other Protestant denominations. He said he couldn't understand how things had gone awry, how a blind spot had developed in the Presbyterian conscience.

> Freedom became my freedom, not yours. I must be free to have a job, have a house, fly a flag, take my procession into your estate. But what about the others? Haven't they an inalienable right to a house, a job, a flag, a pipe band? That's the lesson Ulster Protestants have found hard to learn – and I speak as an Ulster Protestant ...

Rev. Boyd was so right. Freedom is not freedom if it isn't shared with my neighbour.

Reluctantly, we'll leave Cave Hill, but before I ever learned of its historical significance, this was a most wonderful place to me in my youth. I was away above the city, nearly floating like that barn owl, near the clouds, closer to heaven – well at least eleven hundred feet closer!

Before we leave the Cave Hill area I must recall a famous house that became a great cultural centre in its day. This was Ard Righ, the home of a remarkably generous and open-minded man – the writer Francis Joseph Biggar. He encouraged young writers and musicians – anyone who was trying to advance Irish consciousness. He wasn't trying to convert anyone to nationalism, but was simply trying to remind them of their heritage. People like Eoin MacNeill, Roger Casement and Bulmer Hobson came to Ard Righ. Joseph Campbell loved him – 'the lordliest type of Irishman it has ever been my luck to meet'. Someone else described him as a 'Franciscan Presbyterian' – he had statues of Our Lady and St Francis in his garden. He had an insatiable desire to see his country improved. He didn't give a damn about your politics – just don't allow things to fall into ruin. To that end he restored several buildings. Such a generous, giving man. There was never a hard word spoken against him – not very usual in Belfast.

Here we are at Belfast Docklands, looking back at the giant Harland and Wolff cranes 'Samson' and 'Goliath', straddling the River Lagan. In my youth, this was the great

industrial heart of Belfast, captured by Richard Rowley in
his poem 'The Islandmen':

> Terrible as an army with banners
> Through the dusk of a winter's eve
> Over the bridge
> The thousands tramp ...
> And some are old
> Gaunt, grey-bearded, stooped
> With many years of toil, but undejected
> Still they are proud ...

Davy Hammond wrote a wonderful history of the shipyard
workers with the great title *Steel Chest, Nail in the Boot and the
Barking Dog*. One of the great sights for me in the thirties was
to see that 'terrible army' come out of here in the evening.
The trams would rattle out, not just full of workers but
festooned with them, like a swarm of bees, tens of thousands
of them – an extraordinary sight.

My only real connection with the docks is my grandfather
telling me he came here when the *Titanic* and the *Olympic*
were being built. He was Robert Gageby, an ordinary
working man's Labour activist, who fought as secretary of
the Flaxdressers Association for better conditions for all
his people. He was a member of the corporation but when
he went for election to Westminster, everything descended
on him. The papers warned that he could be leading the
decent people of Belfast down the road to Communism
... Unbelievable stuff about non-smoking, non-drinking,

church-going, pious Robert Gageby! He spoke here to the
shipyard workers but they didn't come out for him. He
polled 3,951 votes against the Unionist opponent's 6,275.
The *Northern Whig* reported that the Unionists 'had an
endless stream of motors, broughams and jaunting cars to
get the voters out'. Such was the politics of Belfast at the
time.

Down here in central Belfast there was a marvellous
place called Smithfield. My memories of it are connected
with books and bookshops, especially those of Harry Hall
and Hugh Grier. They had acres of books going for little or
nothing. I remember buying a set of Disraeli's *Curiosities of
Literature* here. I regularly come across books at home that I
bought here for threepence or sixpence. Davy McClean had
a little left-wing bookshop that I frequented also.

I reject the notion of Belfast as a dour old industrial city.
It is a great literary centre – think of MacNeice, Hewitt,
Longley, Mahon, Muldoon, Moore. And it's an artistic centre
– think of Paul Henry, Gerry Dillon, George Campbell,
Andrew Nicholl, Colin Midleton and William Conor –
poor Willie whom I got to know well and who for most of
his life got less than an agricultural wage. Hewitt wrote
a wonderfully prophetic poem in 1969, 'The Coasters', in
which he indicted middle-class indifference to the problems
of Belfast.

> You coasted along
> To larger houses, gadgets, more machines,
> To golf and weekend bungalows,

Caravans when the children were small,
The Mediterranean, later, with the wife
And all the time though you never noticed
The old lies festered,
The ignorant became more thoroughly infected.

The cloud of infection hangs over the city
A quick change of wind and it
Might spill over the leafy suburbs.
You coasted too long.

The difficulty in Northern Ireland is getting people to live together. We're back to the 'pan-Christian front'. Louis MacNeice's father made some wonderful speeches and sermons on this theme in the thirties. His books of collected sermons and speeches are full of kindness and Christian goodness. I read and reread them regularly. And his son sums it all up in two lines:

Put up what flag you like
It's too late to save your soul with bunting.

Gallipoli

A personal visit to the scene of a World War I disaster.

It is a grey November day in 2014. I am with a tour party in a coach that is negotiating the winding wooded slopes along a peninsula in Western Turkey. Ninety-nine years earlier a fellow Meathman was heading for the same destination. He travelled in a troopship as part of the Tenth Division of the British Army. It was July 1915. His name was Francis Ledwidge, a poet and a dreamer, as well as a soldier. The Tenth Division was headed for Gallipoli on the western side of the Dardanelles Peninsula in Turkey, the scene of bitter fighting for the previous three months. Turkey had aligned with Germany in the Great War and was preventing the Allies' ships from progressing through the Dardanelles Straits towards Russia. A decision was made to take the Dardanelles by land from the west. It was to prove a disastrous decision, not one of the finest hours of the first Lord of the Admiralty, Winston Churchill.

The main attack on Gallipoli was led by the ANZAC forces from Australia and New Zealand. We disembark from the coach at Anzac Cove. A first glimpse of the terrain tells how impossible was the task that confronted the Allied forces. Towering above the landing coves were craggy hills from which relentless Turkish rifle and shellfire poured.

Little wonder that the Allies had made scant progress in the three months previous to the Tenth Division's arrival.

In August 1915, Ledwidge and his comrades landed at Suvla Bay on the Gallipoli Peninsula. It was hell from day one. Under a constant barrage from the Turkish snipers, the Allied troops had also to contend with the intense Mediterranean heat, inefficient leadership and all around them the stench of unburied bodies. They developed the 'Gallipoli stoop' from having to crouch constantly under cover. They outnumbered the Turks, but the natives had the advantage of knowledge of the terrain and used it to deadly effect. The Tenth Division had over five thousand casualties in one day for the gain of just one Turkish trench.

And so our 2014 tour becomes a succession of war cemeteries, mainly those of the Anzac forces. Young men – boys of eighteen and nineteen – felled and lost far, far from home. Row after row of white crosses with the minimal information – name, age, regiment. Occasionally a poignant quote from grieving parents – 'He gave his faded brown coat for one of glorious white …' And of course these graves represent only a fraction of the fallen, estimated to be about one hundred and twenty thousand from both sides. At the top of Anzac Cove a huge memorial stone commemorates the dead with the gracious words of the Turkish leader Kemal Ataturk who rose to prominence in the Dardanelles Campaign:

> Those heroes that shed their blood and lost their lives – you are now lying in the soil of a friendly country.

Therefore rest in peace. There is no difference between the Johnnies and the Mehmets to us where they lie side by side here in this country of ours. You the mothers who sent their sons from far away countries, wipe away your tears. Your sons are now lying in our bosom and are in peace. After having lost their lives on this land, they have become our sons as well.

Our coach winds its way upwards towards one of the higher points of Gallipoli. Our guide indicates the remains of opposing trenches. At some points they were only ten to twenty metres apart. There are stories of 'gifts' being lobbed over from one side to the other – tobacco, fruit, etc. – before the killing would resume. The utter lunacy of war. For Francis Ledwidge, it became at once a horrific and an exhilarating experience. He wrote of it to his patron and fellow soldier, Lord Dunsany:

It is surprising what silly things one thinks of in a big fight. I was lying on one side of a low bush on 19 August, pouring lead into the Turks and for four hours my mind was on the silliest things of home. Once I found myself wondering if a cow that I knew to have a disease called 'timbertongue' had really died. Again, a man on my right who was mortally hit said 'It can't be far off now' and I began to wonder what it was could not be far off. Then I knew it was death and I kept repeating the dying man's words: 'It can't be far off now.'

But when the Turks began to retreat I realised my position and, standing up, I shouted out the range to the men near me and they fell like grass before the scythe, the enemy. It was Hell! Hell! No man thought he would ever return. Just fancy – out of D Company, two hundred and fifty strong, only seventy-six returned. By Heavens, you should know the bravery of these men! Cassidy, standing on a hill with his cap on top of his rifle, shouting at the Turks to come out; stretcher-bearers taking in friend and enemy alike. It was a horrible and a great day. I would not have missed it for worlds.

The lunacy of war. The Turkish retreat would be short-lived, however, and gradually the impossibility of the situation dawned on the Allied leaders. A bitter winter had set in. General Hamilton, the commander-in-chief, was recalled. In December 1915 the evacuation of the Tenth Division began and was successfully completed within a month. The retreat was a success but the invasion had been a disaster. Nineteen thousand of Ledwidge's comrades in the Tenth Division had died. He himself survived but he would die eighteen months later in the Third Battle of Ypres.

Our tour ends at the huge memorial to Ataturk, overlooking a foggy Suvla Bay. Our guide has some parting advice for us. 'There is a souvenir shop at the bottom of the hill but if you want a real souvenir, take a stone from the beach!' I take his advice and pick an ochre and white heart-shaped stone at Anzac Cove.

We resume our tour. Destination Istanbul – a five-hour journey on a murky evening through a drab countryside. I grasp the Gallipoli stone tightly, then release it and roll it around in my palm. Thoughts, images come to mind. Later they will crystallise into words ...

I see the stones
Spattered with the blood of youth
Who once again
Were denied the truth.
I see the cliffs above their heads
Impossible to scale
The relentless Turkish guns
Tear those young men to shreds.

I smell the acrid cordite fumes
Seeping through explosive plumes
Total confusion, total slaughter.
And the stench of shattered bodies
Floating bloated
In Aegean water.

I hear the whistle and the thud
Of rifle and of shell
In the mayhem of this manmade hell
I hear the screams
The carnage will not smother
And somewhere a dying Aussie lad
Cries out for his distant mother.

Don Baker
on Daingean Reformatory

Musician and actor Don Baker was sent to Daingean Reformatory in County Offaly at the age of thirteen 'for petty offences'. In 2000 he paid a return visit with me to the now derelict reformatory.

I was brought to this remote place as a frightened youngster. I still remember that day, being taken away from my family in Dublin. I was escorted down on a bus by a Garda. Initially I was handcuffed to him but he removed the handcuffs on the promise that I wouldn't run away. I kept my promise.

My first emotion on seeing these grey walls is anger, extreme anger. It's also an eerie feeling as I enter the building. I can see the same paint on the walls, forty years later. I spent two years of my life here with a couple of hundred young lads. It was a grim place …

Here we are in the refectory where we had our meals. A bit like a dungeon, with a vaulted ceiling. It was like a scene from *Oliver*. The food was appalling. For breakfast you got a quarter loaf with a lump of margarine stuck on it. Tea was served from a bucket. A lad would scoop the tea into tin mugs. Dinner was a tray of often rotten potatoes with a kind of goulash. And a dessert of pink, lumpy custard. Tea was the same as breakfast. The brother on duty would walk up and down saying his Rosary. After about six months the food improved somewhat. I remember getting into a scrap with another boy. I was grabbed by the hair coming in here and put kneeling in the corner. No tea or bread that evening. A weird place.

We rose at six o'clock each morning. The brother would come in with a big stick, shouting 'Back-street curs! Out of bed! Back-street curs!' He would lash the legs off you if you didn't get out quickly enough. We washed with cold water and that red scrubbing soap. A lot of lads suffered from scurvy due to the lack of nutrition, but there was no treatment for it. You just lived with it. Then Mass in the chapel and out to the yard for up to an hour. Then you were summoned to breakfast by the clapping of hands. There were no verbal orders – everything was done to the clapping of hands. After breakfast, out to the yard for another half-hour before setting off on work detail, which could be on the farm, in the shoe shop, in the garden or on the bog. Working on the bog was tough, but good fun. I still have the scars from catching and barrowing the turf. A break for dinner and then back to work. There was also a woodwork room run by Mr Whitty, a very compassionate man – one of the few nice people here. Unfortunately, I was never much good at woodwork.

This is the main stairwell and it was here at the bottom of the stairs that they would flog us if we did anything wrong. 'Wrong' might be getting into a fight with another lad. You would kneel on the first step and stretch your hands to maybe the third step. A brother would stand on your fingers so you couldn't move. Another brother administered the 'punishment' with a leather strap. You were beaten from the knees up – your legs would look like the lines on a blackboard, with blood coming from little pinholes. Your body went into spasm as the sting of the leather went through it. You wouldn't know when the next blow would come. I made a big mistake. I didn't cry. I went into therapy for years afterwards. They beat us here because the dormitories were directly above us. The other boys would hear every blow and every scream of terror. One boy's beating affected everybody. It was quite an ordeal. I called this place 'Little Auschwitz' – a prison for little kids.

The dormitory was L-shaped, with four rows of beds on either side. I was lucky – my bed was beside a radiator. A night watchman sat all night at a desk with a little light on it. He came in from the town. The night I got the beating I had to kneel on the bed for a couple of hours because of the pain. The night watchman came up to me and handed me a fork with a piece of liver on it. 'Here you are, son. Eat that!' he said. I suppose it was his way of saying sorry …

There were some bright moments but there was little enough to brighten the day. You could play football or handball and hopefully forget what was going on around you. When it rained they put us in the recreation hall where you just sat around and played cards or 'jackstones'. On Sundays we had a lie-in until eight o'clock, but otherwise it was much the same as other days. Instead of work, you went around the yard all day. There was no contact with the town outside. It was a very boring day. You could only play so much handball. A letter from my Mum would be a highlight. It would be opened and censored – and if you were lucky there might be a few bob inside.

We are now entering the chapel. One of my jobs was to ring the Angelus at twelve and at six. Three threes and a nine! Every time I pulled the rope I'd get a shower of straw from the bell-tower! I worked here in the chapel for over a year. I have horrible memories of this place. Cleaning and dusting every day, but there is only so much dusting you can do. Most of the time I would sit here and just daydream. My nerves would be wrecked here, every day on my own. It was so quiet. The words *Sanctus, Sanctus, Sanctus* are still on the wall but this was no sanctuary for me. I remember one morning a boy began to fall asleep at Mass. The priest came down from the altar and began to beat him around the place and call him names. Another time we were all ushered in here on a Saturday afternoon. We didn't know what to expect. The priest strode up into the pulpit, took off his spectacles and began thumping the Bible and screaming about the evil of masturbation, 'wasting the seed of life', as he called it. They were paranoid about masturbation. I was queried about it in the office the first day I arrived here. This priest then told us a scary story about a boy who took ill and died because of masturbation. It is so funny now but at the time we were terrified.

Here in the sacristy, a brother accused me of kissing another boy in the handball alley. I denied it. He hit me across the face with the leather. 'Tell me the truth!' I denied it again. He hit me again. 'I believe you. You are a good boy!' I vomited into the wash-handbasin.

And finally the visiting room. We could play ping pong here. Look! There are Christmas decorations on the wall still! And cobwebs everywhere. Cobwebs of memory! In many ways I am the person I am because of the experiences I had in this place. I have tried to live without regret. I'd like to take some positive meaning out of the experience. I'm even grateful for some aspects of it! It woke me up. Even if that one thing came out of it, that's good enough for me.

I remember the day I left. The brother put me on the bus to Dublin. I turned and said to him 'I'll pray for you'. I wasn't being sarcastic – the words just came out of my mouth. The brother said nothing. There was a song going around in my head ... Simon and Garfunkel's 'Homeward Bound'.

Muriel and Narcissus

In 1995, Muriel McCarthy, Keeper of Marsh's Library, Dublin, the oldest public library in Ireland, enthused about the library and its founder Narcissus Marsh.

Narcissus Marsh was an extraordinary man – a brilliant scholar, a provost of Trinity College, Dublin, an Archbishop of Cashel, of Dublin and of Armagh and – most importantly for me – the founder of this wonderful library.

He was born in 1638 in Hannington, Wiltshire, and educated at Oxford. If you think his Christian name was odd, he had two brothers named Epaphroditus and Onesiphorus! When the bishop who gave him his first parish expected him to marry the daughter of a friend, Marsh was outraged and returned to Oxford where he acquired a doctorate and held various offices. He was approached in 1679 by the Duke of Ormonde who offered him the Provostship of Trinity College, Dublin, on the strength of Marsh's proven administrative ability. Marsh accepted and was sworn in as Provost of the three-hundred-and-forty-student university. He was a severe man of strong views. He didn't have a great opinion of the students in his care. He records in his diary, 'I am weary of this lewd and debauched town, whereby the students are both ignorant and rude.'

Because of his scholarship, he was very interested in libraries. He noticed that only staff and students had access to the library of Trinity College – it being a private institution – and thought it a frightful disadvantage that a capital city had no library for the public. In this area alone – the Liberties of Dublin – you would have had an educated population of rich merchants (including Huguenots), army personnel, administrators, clergymen, doctors and other professional men. Marsh's prime motivation was to provide a library for such people, and this became feasible on his appointment as Archbishop of Dublin in 1694 – an appointment that brought him the wealth to undertake the project.

The library was designed by Sir William Robinson, who also designed the Royal Hospital in Kilmainham. Work began in 1701 and was completed in 1707 with the library's incorporation in a government 'Act for Settling and Preserving a Public Library Forever' – the first such library in Ireland, and still going strong nearly three hundred years later. The library is actually on the first floor, which would not be uncommon in those times. They were very conscious of damp and the nearby River Poddle was prone to flooding. And of course the ground floor provided a residence for the librarian, for which I am personally grateful to Narcissus!

Entering the library on the first floor is like walking back in time. So little has changed, thankfully. The beautiful oak cases are so simple and elegant. There is a window for every stack, offering the only light for reading at that time. There is the lovely plaque to help you find the books – beautifully ornamented with the archbishop's mitre on top. The library was cleverly designed in an L-shape, with the librarian's desk at the apex – to keep an eye on both galleries. In this first gallery, the books were originally chained for security purposes. You can still see the remains of the locks at the edges of the bookcases. The books were originally catalogued by author and are still in the same place with the same class number. Apart from the chains and the original benches, nothing has changed. There are so few buildings in Dublin that were designed for a specific purpose and are still used for that purpose.

Marsh eventually amassed some twenty-five thousand volumes. He bought the Bishop of Worcester's private library for two and a half thousand pounds, something that caused great distress in England as that had been regarded as the finest private library in that country. We have an extremely good collection of books on Ireland here, but what Marsh assembled was a great European library, representing the outstanding ideas of the seventeenth and eighteenth centuries: the writings of Newton; advances in medicine; travellers' accounts of newly discovered lands; philosophical ideas like those of Descartes. It is not a 'religious' library, though founded by a religious man and containing many religious volumes. It is really a scholars' library for Renaissance men who had an interest in medicine, science, history, witchcraft, travel, grammars and lexicons. The rule of the library was that you had to be 'a graduate and a gentleman and pay due respect to your elders'.

This was (and is) a scholars' library. The books are leather-bound and have little ornamentation. They are not cosmetic – here for appearance only. These books were used and many of them are annotated with the marginalia of their readers. One of the annotators was Jonathan Swift, who became Dean of St Patrick's across from the library here. Here in Clarendon's *History of Rebellion and Civil Wars of England*, Swift shows his dislike of Scottish people. He underlines the words 'honesty' and 'courage' and writes in the margin – 'trifles to a Scot'. Swift also had an intense dislike of Marsh. He was a student of Marsh in his last year of his provostship and may have been disciplined by the provost. Swift said of Marsh that 'no man will be either glad or sorry at his death, except his successor'. It became personal. 'To sit beside him [Marsh] is not at all a place of honour because of the smell emanating from him …'

Here in the second gallery are the 'cages' with their beautiful Gothic windows. Readers were locked in here to prevent them from stealing the books. The original wirework is still here. We are overlooking the beautiful garden and beyond it the archbishop's palace – now Kevin Street garda station. In the eighteenth century this library was the wonder of the age. For one hundred and fifty years it was the only library available for people to come in and study. The poet and songwriter Thomas Moore would have been a regular user of the library, as would doctors, barristers, clergymen and other professional men. And I say men because there were few if any women to be seen here – maybe Stella (Swift's friend), Mrs Delaney and a few others. Moore in fact asked to be locked in here at night because the opening hours were not long enough for him.

There is such variety here. There's a book by the Dean of Mainz who wrote of his travels to the Holy Land in the fourteenth century. It has a wonderful panorama of Venice which opens out of the book – a woodcut printed on a little wooden printing press. It is one of our treasures. The oldest book we have is Cicero's *Letters to Friends*, printed in Milan in 1472. And here is Bishop Leslie's *History of Scotland*, published in 1578. It has the earliest known medallion portrait of Mary Queen of Scots and her son James I. All of these books are in Latin (the international language), which meant they were quickly available to Marsh. He didn't have to wait around for translations and he was in regular correspondence with booksellers and writers. Here is a book showing 'a list of popish parish priests in counties throughout the kingdom of Ireland, 1705'. For example, it tells us that Fr Kelly of Ballinakill in Iar-Chonnacht was fifty years old and received orders from James Lynch, Titular Bishop of Tuam. And finally, here on the librarian's desk, is a beautiful book bound in green vellum. It is Marsh's Donations Book, which accounts in detail for all the gifts made to the library in books or money. The very first book donated is the Holy Bible (London, 1701) given by the Most Reverend Father in God, Dr Thomas Tennyson, Lord Archbishop of Canterbury – and of course that book is still here.

For some time, Marsh employed his niece Grace as his housekeeper but, unfortunately for him, Grace fell in love with a young clergyman, Charles Proby, and eloped with him. Marsh records in his diary that 'this evening betwixt eight and nine of the clock, my niece Grace, not having the fear of God in front of her eyes, stole privately out of my house and was this night married to Charles Proby and was bedded there with him in a tavern in Castleknock. Lord consider my affliction!' The scandal of it all! Grace is said to have regretted her action and left a letter to her uncle in one of the books. Marsh's ghost is said to haunt the library looking for the letter. I've never seen the ghost – nor have I found the letter!

Marsh died in 1713 and is buried just beside the library in the grounds of St Patrick's Cathedral. Inside the cathedral there is a fine monument to him, the work of Grinling Gibbons.

Yes, Narcissus Marsh was a severe, serious and probably a dull man. He did play the lute, but each time he did he would say 'O God forgive me for this vain waste of time'! But I think Swift was most unfair to him. Marsh was a brilliant scholar and a deeply religious man – 'a godly man'. He led an upright and honest life, which couldn't be said about a lot of the clergy at that time. Here was a man who had a dream of providing a city (which was not his own) with a great library for people to visit as they wished to study the great ideas of the time. He then spent every penny he had on realising that dream. Indeed the library was not initially named after him. It was called the Library of St Sepulchre. On the whole this was a most generous and very admirable man – and certainly I'm grateful to him!

John Lonergan

on Mountjoy Prison

In 2000, the then Governor of Mountjoy Prison in Dublin, John Lonergan, guided me through the prison and reflected on the workings and the efficacy of the prison system.

We are standing just inside the main gate of Mountjoy Prison. In one hundred and fifty years of operation, over half a million people have come through that gate. Even to come here as a visitor, there is something eerie about the slap of that gate behind you. There is the realisation that you are confined, no more free to come and go as you please. I will take you through the prison now, as if you were a newly arrived prisoner. We enter the general office where you will give information about your home address, age, background, medical condition. You will hand over your personal property – whatever money you have, your watch, rings, etc., which will be held for you until your release. Your money will be credited to your account in the 'tuckshop'.

Next we move to the reception area, where you are processed – you hand up your clothes, have a shower, have body marks and scars noted, are searched for contraband (drugs), are weighed and given prison clothing. You may later get your own clothing back if you so wish, but it is checked and you get it at your own risk. Just across from here is the visiting area and you can hear the sound of babies and small children. It's a sad indicator of the isolation that prison brings. You will be entitled to one family visit of thirty minutes per week, under supervision, so it is very difficult to have any privacy – one of the many aspects of the punishment of prison.

We now move into the circle – a busy, noisy place as the prisoners move about. Someone once described it as being like Heuston Station, but if you consider that there can be close to one thousand people here – seven hundred prisoners and three hundred custodial and support staff – it is the equivalent of a small town in a confined space. The circle is the hub of the prison, which is modelled on the old Pentonville system – a circle with four wings radiating from it. In the old days, the idea was that the governor and chief officer could command the prison from here. Here still is the famous triangle that Brendan Behan wrote and sang about ...

> A hungry feelin' came o'er me stealin'
> And the mice were squealin' in me prison cell
> And that ould triangle went jingle jangle
> Along the banks of the Royal Canal.

It's redundant now, of course, replaced by radio and electronic communication, but in Behan's time especially in the still of the morning it was a very effective way of calling the prisoners [*he rings the triangle to illustrate this*]. There was no great innovation in naming the four wings here – they were named A, B, C and

D, with three landings on each wing, accommodating up to one hundred and thirty people per wing.

We are now at the 'tuckshop', where prisoners can purchase cigarettes, sweets, biscuits or soft drinks out of their own money plus a gratuity of a pound per day which they receive here. It gives them a little bit of control over their lives. Previously they put in an order that was delivered to their cells. It's a busy place today because they are stocking up for the weekend. Again, it's the equivalent of the village shop for a small town.

We are now in D wing, where I believe Behan spent most of his time. At the far end is the old execution chamber, so it's a historic part of the prison, where much suffering was endured. There's a lot of opening and closing of doors to get through the prison. You would probably notice it more than we do! Generally, prison operates smoothly. There isn't a huge amount of security visible. There are a lot of young men in Mountjoy. Research done in 1997 showed that the average prisoner age was twenty-seven, but a huge number ranged between eighteen and twenty-five. A particularly depressing statistic revealed that 77 per cent of the prisoners had previously served time in St Patrick's Detention Centre for sixteen to twenty-one-year-olds. That indicates that prison on its own doesn't work. It is very hard to break away from recidivism. Only 6 per cent of prisoners stay on at school after age sixteen, whereas the norm outside is 80 per cent.

Worldwide, the same type of people end up in prison. It indicates the imbalances in society, the role that class plays in a person's life. Many of these prisoners were destined for crime. There are six relatively small pockets of Dublin that supply 75 per cent of the city's prisoners. There are roads in Dublin where nearly every family is represented in Mountjoy. Many of these prisoners have committed serious crimes, but others are as much victims of circumstances as the victims they have created. In addition to social circumstances, a huge percentage have behavioural and psychiatric difficulties. They find it difficult to integrate with society. Contrary to popular perception, few of these prisoners are well off due to crime. Maybe 1 per cent are making money. The vast majority are penniless, which indicates an inability to manage money. They squander money when they have it. So, many of them are not just failed criminals – they are not successful at anything.

That's why it's gratifying to see them benefit from our projects here – the Connect (Awareness) Project, the drama productions. They have talents, but often these lie dormant for many years. Growing up, they were not exposed to the challenges and opportunities that others were. That's why we need to get the message out to children in the trouble 'pockets' that education has meaning and value. Otherwise we are repeating the cycle and you will have three generations of criminals passing through here.

Another area of skill training is here in the kitchen. This is a purpose-built area with a bakery underneath, which bakes for all the Dublin prisons. The kitchen is a major operation, providing seven hundred meals four times a day which are delivered to each wing. It has won a Q mark for quality for the last three years, getting 96 to 97 per cent for quality, hygiene and preparation. If offers an invaluable skill for use outside. We also have education projects with teachers from the City of Dublin VEC offering a wide range of classes in literacy, computers, languages and the arts. When the food is delivered, the prisoner collects his meal and returns to the cell. There is unfortunately no communal dining in Mountjoy. It is an unnatural way of doing things. If you are here for five or six years and you are released into society, then to go out, sit and dine with others is totally alien to you. It is institutionalisation at is worst.

We are under extreme pressure for space here. These cells – twelve feet by six feet with one barred window – were intended for one individual, but nowadays you have a bunk bed for two in most cells. Outside we used to have a market garden area, a grass patch and a handball alley, but they were all built on to provide the training unit, the healthcare unit and so on, so we ended up with a concrete jungle within the walls of Mountjoy. There are no grass areas. This exercise yard caters for A wing and part of B wing, so you could have up to two hundred people using it at a time. Most just walk around. A few may try to play football.

What was called the hospital wing is now called the separation unit. As the name implies, it is intended for men who need to be kept separate from the main prison population – because of the crimes they have committed (e.g. sex offenders) or they may be at risk, owing money for drugs, etc. It is a major problem for us to protect people in this unit from other prisoners. We could have up to fifty people here at any one time.

Prison is a tough place, made tougher by the fact that this is an old and in some ways outdated building. You are isolated from your loved ones, your freedom is curtailed and you have little privacy. On top of all that we have a major problem with drugs. They are very difficult to find and eliminate. The users have invariably come from areas where drugs are already a problem. Addiction is a scourge, especially with heroin which is predominantly done by injection, leading to further health problems.

So now as we complete our tour, John, and we open the gate to let you back out into the world, you'll give a sigh of relief when you hear the slap of that gate – from the outside!

Ballyfin

On 1 May 2011, Ballyfin in County Laois opened its doors as an exclusive hotel after years of restoration. It had previously been a boarding school for seventy years. I spent five years as a boarder in the then Patrician College, Ballyfin, in the 1950s and later made an award-winning radio documentary about that experience. I returned to Ballyfin in 2011 as a paying guest.

The gates were locked. How often during our boarding school days, fifty-plus years ago, would we have wished to be confronted with this sight. With, hopefully, a notice affixed: PLAGUE, KEEP OUT or SCHOOL CLOSED DUE TO FIRE.

Patrician College, Ballyfin, County Laois, had been our 'home' for five years in the fifties. Originally the home of the Coote family, the six-hundred-acre estate and mansion had been bought for £10,000 in 1929 by the Patrician Brothers, who ran it as a boarding school for the next seven decades. In 2002 American business magnate Fred Krehbiel bought the entire estate and set about restoring it to its nineteenth-century splendour. In 2009 the school closed, to be merged into a new community school in Mountrath.

Five years ago, as the restoration began, fellow past pupil Colman Morrissey and I made a vow that whenever Ballyfin reopened as a luxury hotel (as was Krehbiel's plan) we would come back as guests, no matter what the cost. I had made an award-winning radio documentary on my Ballyfin years two decades previously, so this would be an especially emotional 'homecoming'. And now the gates were locked.

The delay was minimal. As soon as we announced ourselves on the intercom, the gates swung open and we drove up the long, winding avenue through the bluebell woods until the imposing Palladian mansion was revealed in the May sunshine.

> He was fearful. He had left the familiarity and security of home in a small village in County Meath, sixty miles away. The Ford Prefect rattled over the cattle grid. Goodbye, it seemed to say. Goodbye to his friends, his parents. Goodbye to the world. Four great columns guarded the entrance doors where the president, Br Silverius, stood greeting the parents ...*

The entire management team came out to welcome us. We were, after all, the first paying guests on this historic opening day of Ballyfin Hotel. A valet took our cars away. We move through the entrance hall with its intricately patterned mosaic floor – brought from Italy in 1822 – and into the sumptuous saloon, dominated by four dark green *scagliola* columns. This great room, with its rich plasterwork and coved ceiling, was designed to receive distinguished company and exudes warmth and hospitality. We, returned

---

* Note: All quotations are from the original radio documentary: *Ballyfin – A Boarding School Memory.*

twenty-first-century exiles, are indeed made to feel distinguished as we sip a welcoming coffee and absorb the grandeur around us. It is a truly emotional experience.

The accommodation manager shows us around the rooms that are available. Fifty years ago these would have been the brothers' rooms, sparely furnished with a bed, chair, wardrobe and little else. Now they are restored to nineteenth-century splendour. Nothing has been spared in terms of furnishings, paintings and decor. It is all captured in Kevin Mulligan's lavish coffee-table book – *Ballyfin: The Restoration of an Irish House and Demesne* – published by the owner as a testament to the work done on this great house – and a thing of great beauty in itself.

There is good news. Because the hotel isn't fully booked, we can have a room each rather than share. Colman will enjoy the Mountrath Room and, to his great envy, I acquire the Wellesley Pole Suite, named after William Wellesley, older brother of the Duke of Wellington, who inherited Ballyfin in 1781. I defend my right of acquisition through my Meath connection to Wellington. A whole suite to myself – luxurious sitting room, elegant bedroom and imposing bathroom. I could get used to this.

> He awoke to a new and strange world. Brother Angelus marched through the dormitory, ringing a handbell. It was so unusual to find himself sharing a room with fifty other boys. The hubbub and clamour grew as the washroom filled up and boys queued for handbasins. He washed quickly. The towel smelled of home ...

A further delight awaits when I consider the view from my suite. A magnificent cascade tumbles musically down the sloping grounds from beneath a Claudian temple. This concept, the creation of Jim Reynolds, director of the restoration project, is at once breathtaking and soothing to ear and eye, adding a wondrous centrepiece to what the Cootes would have known as the Pleasure Grounds. They had been our restricted 'pleasure grounds' too ...

> If you didn't play games, you went for walks in the grounds, remembering always to stay within bounds – *Ne ambulaveritis in horto, pueri* (Do not walk in the garden, boys). The gardens with their orchard were out of bounds, as were the lake and the tower. Some boys were very daring and would go out over the demesne wall to Delaney's shop, or worse still to Phelan's pub ...

Settled into our rooms, we begin to familiarise ourselves with the house. Down the beautiful cantilevered Portland stone stairway and through the stair hall, now hung with Coote family portraits that have been diligently traced and restored to the house after a century's absence – a measure of the meticulous work that has gone into its restoration. Across the saloon and through the rotunda – for me, one of the gems of Ballyfin, with its eight Sienna marble columns, its intricate plasterwork dome and its stunning inlaid floor, which Kevin Mulligan informs us 'became the extraordinary setting for a magic railway, as the Coote children used to set up their model trains after tea on wet afternoons'. The rotunda is a link room to the library.

This magnificent room with its many mahogany-fronted bookcases and deep bowed window is typical of great eighteenth-century houses, originally a male preserve but latterly more of a family living room. With matching Morrison chimneypieces at either end, it exudes warmth and restfulness in the company of books. Books are generously displayed for the entertainment of the modern traveller in the restored Ballyfin, with a warning on each bookplate: 'Consider it the vilest sin, to steal a book from Ballyfin'!

Mr O'Reilly asked himself and Tim Dunne to help with the cataloguing of books in the library. It was a pleasant change to be released from the study hall to work in the beautiful library. It was good to handle books, to feel their bindings, to turn their often-delicate leaves and to wonder at the strangeness of their titles – *Masterpieces of Eloquence, Outlines of Dogmatic Theory, The Catechism of Perseverance Vols. 1–4.*

One bookcase in the library is a disguised door that leads into the conservatory. This masterpiece, designed by Richard Turner, had fallen into decay despite the best efforts of Br Joseph and a FÁS team in the 1990s to repair it. It is important to record that in their seventy-year tenure of Ballyfin, the Patrician Brothers did their utmost to preserve the house but, with meagre resources, it was always an uphill battle. Lunch will be served in the conservatory

today. Excellent idea! With the assistance of the two Freds
– Executive Chef Fred Cordonnier (ex-Patrick Guilbaud)
and Food and Beverage Manager Frederic Poivre – we
make our choices. We both opt for warm asparagus salad,
guinea fowl egg and pata negra ham to start. My main
course is pan-fried fillet of sea bass, pickled spring carrots,
and coriander yoghurt. Colman prefers pan-fried rib eye of
beef, green beans, potato lyonnaise and béarnaise sauce. Ah
this is the life, Colman. Do you remember the old days?

> The food was sparse. Tea, bread and butter in the
> evening, with a spoonful of jam on Fridays and
> Sundays. Someone at the table might have a tin of beans
> or sardines and if he was lucky, they might share ... On
> Sunday morning there was a sausage for breakfast –
> which was fine if he hadn't actually lost it (or even a
> whole term's sausages) at cards or push-ha'penny ...

Suitably replenished, we decide to remove ourselves to the
pleasure grounds to take some fresh air. We make a detour
through the splendid Gold Room, originally the ladies'
'drawing room'. They laughed at us fifty years ago when we
came home on holiday and told of a room adorned with gilt
mirrors, gilded plasterwork and silk-covered walls, but it was
true. We had been there and seen it, admittedly only during
the retreat, when Fr Sebastian heard our confessions there ...

> Fr Sebastian gave talks on Bad Actions, Bad Thoughts,
> Bad Language ... There were sniggers from the seniors

at the back of the oratory. If you were really worried about something, you could drop a question into the Question Box. Larry O'Gorman didn't need a Question Box. He stood up bravely and asked: 'Is it a sin to call a brother a fool?'

A long ramble would do us both good but we take the lazy twenty-first century option and employ a golf buggy to get us around. Well there is so much to *see* ... the restored walled garden, the tower (which we can enter to enjoy the spectacular views of the midlands), the fernery (I never knew we had a fernery) and the lake – all out-of-bounds territory in days of old. The football pitches are just grassland now. And there where the goal mouth was, scene of many a melee, is a giant H – the helicopter pad. The semi-demolished handball alleys are derelict. It transpires that the alleys were built on the original wall of the grapery.

> Reputations and fortunes – of sausages and even cigarettes – were won and lost in the alleys. Pudsy Ryan was the King of the Alleys. Nobody stood a chance with Pudsy. He could 'butt' a ball with deadly accuracy.

The trip around the lake affords us the opportunity to see Ballyfin in all its glory – a majestic thirteen-bay mansion bathed in May sunshine.

A swim would be nice before dinner – not in the lake, but in the state-of-the-art swimming pool. In 1930 the Brothers

built a four-storey block, which was essentially the school.
The basement was our refectory. Now it is a swimming pool. I
relax there in peaceful solitude.

> The boys lined up before charging downstairs to
> the refectory. Each table had a prefect and two sub-
> prefects in charge of giving out the food. The 'ref' was
> noisy and boisterous.

Wait a minute! There's something different about this school
block. It's only three storeys high! As part of the restoration,
the top floor (our dormitory) was shaved off to align it with
the height of the mansion ... Most of our life as students was
confined to that 'modern' block. Our main contact with the
mansion was through our twice-daily visits to the oratory.

> Each pew had a series of white enamel numbers affixed
> to it. Later, he would learn how to unscrew the number
> with a nail file, insert a message behind the number and
> screw it back on. In this way he would be remembered
> in fifty years time, maybe forever ...

The oratory was originally the state dining room and now
it has been tastefully restored to that original function (I
wonder where my pew is now). We repair there for dinner
after a most convivial reception in the library – champagne
with lobster and foie gras canapes. (Well, it's a change from
the usual Sunday evening spoon of jam ...). Once again,
the two Freds do us proud. My entree is a terrine of quail,

organic chicken, foie gras mousse, cherry fig, melba toast and port syrup. The plat de resistance is pan-roasted fillet of Hereford beef, oxtail and foie gras celeriac puree, red onion and creamed potato. With two most palatable wines, I can just about entertain the Ballyfin 'Eton Mess' for dessert.

We repair to the bar for cognacs. The Ballyfin school experience is receding at quite a pace. On the way to the bar, I must answer a call of nature. The location of the toilets is strangely familiar. It can't be. It is. The former president's office where many a trembling misbehaving student had to report. 'Justice!' Colman and I cry in unison.

And so to bed in the Wellesley-Pole Suite, to sleep to the music of the cascade outside, perchance to dream of Br Angelus marching in with bell clanging at 7.30 a.m. No!

A leisurely breakfast at 10 a.m. begins the new day. Schooldays put me off porridge for life. I sample it this morning – a lot more palatable fifty years later, but I am still not convinced ... Papers and morning coffee in the library, as a gentleman does. One more engagement before I leave. I have booked in for a full body massage in the treatment room beside the pool. A full hour of total restoration in what I am told was originally the vegetable store. I am ready for the world.

Leaving Ballyfin was difficult. (Did I ever think I would write that sentence?) This had been an emotional return – a jumble of memories and pleasurable experiences. Five years then. One day now. So much to assimilate and sift. I thought a lot of my parents who had made extraordinary sacrifices to send me and my three siblings to boarding school. I thought of the Patrician Brothers.

The brothers were no fools, whatever Larry O'Gorman thought. They were honest, hardworking countrymen – men with ruddy weather-beaten faces, who might well be his uncles or neighbouring farmers. Men who could turn from teaching Honours Maths to fixing the plumbing. Teachers, bakers, farmers ...

On my way home I would call to pay them my respects in the village cemetery, for they had made sacrifices too – for me and thousands of others.

As for Ballyfin, Fred Krehbiel's vision of restoring a country house has been realised in stunning fashion, and he is to be commended for achieving that in the teeth of a severe recession. It is quite expensive to stay there, but for myself and Colman – returning after over half a century to a very different Ballyfin – the experience was totally worthwhile. Well might we echo the words of Lady Kildare in 1759:

Yesterday I saw a most delightful place indeed, much beyond any place I have seen in Ireland – Ballyfin.

Paddy Graham
on County Westmeath

Artist Paddy Graham returns to childhood locations in County Westmeath where the landscape and the silence had a huge influence on his development as a painter.

> It was the Warm Summer, that landmark
> In a child's mind, an infinite day,
> Sunlight and burnt grass,
> Green grasshoppers on the railway slopes,
> The humming of the wild bees,
> The whole summer during the school holidays
> Till the blackberries appeared.
> Yes, a tremendous time that summer stands
> Beyond the grey finities of normal weather.
>
> (Patrick Kavanagh, 'Living in the Country')

We're here in Streamstown, County Westmeath, a quiet spot in the heart of rural Ireland. This was my grandfather's home. He had a small farm and a plant nursery that stretched over the back of that hill. I came here as a young child in sad circumstances. My father left home and my mother had to care for a young family on her own. It was very difficult for her and she ultimately contracted TB, probably from the stress of it all. The family was split up. I was sent here to live with my grandparents and my uncles, Joe and Tom.

This is a very quiet place, full of wonderful silence. As a child when I came here I was full of loneliness and lostness. I didn't know what to make of being here, surrounded as I was by old people. We're looking across at what used to be a poppy field. I melt into that field when I think of it. I would walk into the middle of it as a child and sit down in this sea of red. I was a tiny child, so the poppies enveloped me in a glistening lime green forest of stalks. I remember that experience with softness and wonder. This was a cinematic dreamworld for me, but even looking at the reality of it now, with the poppies long gone, it is still wonderful. Listen to that apparent silence! There's a dog barking, probably miles away. The crows are shifting in the trees. My paintings come out of silence. There is a moment when painting is no longer an act of doing or making but of receiving. I was and still am an incomplete, unfinished person. There is something irreparable in me. I came up here and still do, for these 'silent' places – that kind of silence where you can hear a fly hopping from one leaf to another, a silence that carried sounds from out of my existence into it. This is where my painting comes from.

This place is full of caves – glades among the trees – which were secret places for me as a child for hiding and listening. I would climb into the trees and talk to them and to myself and look out at the world. The magical shadows and the dappled light were a visual and sensual delight for me. Then I would come out into the open, a stunning, sculptural green as the sun lit up everything. It is an extraordinary landscape of memory for me, while others would pass up and down here day in, day out, without noticing anything. The actual name of this place is Windmill, as there was a wind-powered flax mill here. An old man told my uncle Joe that on the Night of the Big Wind the sails went too fast and the mill went on fire. The stone ruin of it fascinated me and I often tried to draw it. My uncle Joe tells me that as a five- or six-year-old, I was always outside with a copybook, sketching things. Again listen to the 'silence' here! The insects buzzing, our footsteps. How lovely and cool it is in this dappled light. This throws me back into a magical world. This is the background to many of my paintings. This is the richness in those long, empty landscapes I use.

The nursery shed was another magical place. All those shelves with tiny drawers that had brass handles affixed. Inside was an amazing array of seeds. I used to love looking through the envelopes that had wonderful faraway addresses in New Zealand, Australia and other exotic places. There was a local craftsman, Michael Egan, who painted the wood-graining. He would pull hairs from a donkey's tail, tie them to a stick and paint with the most delicate effect. I would stand there, open-mouthed, watching him being absolutely sure of everything he did. He would paint shopfronts in the village and then turn to making a wheel rim for a cart, pull it red-hot from a charcoal fire before shoeing it onto the wheel. To this day I have great love and respect for craftsmanship like that.

There's the old pigsty in the farmyard. I spent a lot of time looking in at and chatting to the pigs. I had a great fondness for them. I hated seeing them killed but I still watched in horror as they were butchered on a table that had already been scrubbed clean with salt. And then there was the surreal killing of the geese. Their heads would be nicked and they bled as they quietly walked around until they dropped to the ground! There used to be a grain store in that loft. Myself and my cousin Pat used to hide in the grain and play tricks on people. I remember how over time the grain would polish the floor of the loft.

This is not nostalgia for the past. This is reality. It belongs to my history, which I don't see as nostalgic at all. It plays a huge part in the way I paint, draw, set up paintings. I set up paintings from a Westmeath point of view, going back to Mullingar where I learned as a teenager, under the tutelage of Dermot Larkin, how to set up a stage in the County Hall and paint backdrops for musical shows. Then in my paintings the Westmeath landscape becomes the stage and I will use either the lake landscape or this very personal, secretive landscape where I talked to the trees. So there's no harking back to better days here. This is cinema to me, like rolling a wonderful movie, a magical dreamlike world. Although I was lonely here, my life is extraordinarily rich because of it, something I picked up on later in London and Dublin, when I rediscovered myself after years of alcoholism and then rediscovered painting. This is what I went back to, this is where I rediscovered the language of landscape.

I followed my grandfather all around the place. He had a great love for the soil. He would reach down into it, pick it up, taste it, grind it in his hand, let it run through his fingers.

He would know if it needed lime or anything. He just had this innate sense, with no need for any measuring tools. This was also, I think, a declaration of ownership on his part. So living here for me was a very full, rich life. Compared to a 'sophisticated' place like Mullingar, this place would seem barren, but you have to grow with it. There is nothing here like Killarney or the Grand Canyon, but this is a lived-in rolled-up landscape that folds in on itself like whipped cream in places. And listen again to the orchestra of sounds in this apparent silence. Nature, earth and sky are united in perfect harmony here.

We have moved a few miles up the road to Monaghanstown Bog. At one level this place speaks to me of hard work, saving the turf with flies and midges bothering me. But in other ways being here was a very personal experience. There was a sense of religion about it. This emerged much later in my life when I was recovering from alcoholism. I became very friendly with Fr Raphael Short. We would discuss theology and philosophy, and he introduced me to the notion of 'throwness' – we are thrown into the world and are caught up in the 'throw' of various moods. When he said that word I was immediately back here, where I felt a very primal experience, of being rooted in this rich, luscious bogland. As a child, everything is at eye-level. I used to stand here and look across the wonderful browns and greens and purples and then on top of that, all those flies and midges!

This horizon became the backdrop for a lot of my work – an exotic view right in the heart of the midlands. I am earthed to here, I belong to here. This is my home. I love the thatch on top of it and the sensual female earth underneath. It may sound odd but this is where I pray, not in words but in wonder about nature. This is where I was thrown back to and thrown out of myself. Being who I am, I am obsessed with myself. This is where I get relief from myself and a sense of otherness – and that is prayer.

Our final location is on the shore of Lough Owel, in the shadow of Captain's Hill. I use water in a symbolic sense in my paintings. I think of the footwashing scene in the Bible and it implies a notion of humility and honour. Or handwashing, which I have used a number of times and which implies betrayal. I recall being in a mental hospital and sensing the betrayal of other patients when people came in and laughed at them. Captain's Hill has a look of Calvary about it. I have used it to symbolise suffering and pain. Jung has said that if you sit and contemplate an image for long enough in silence, there is a kind of moving down into oneself and into echoes of other things. I used to come here a lot, specifically to do that. In these parts of Westmeath, this was the nearest I ever got to feeling complete. Something will always be out of reach, but that is glorious. I would hate things to be 'finished'. I love these places where you are thrown out of yourself – out of the concerns with 'mean living', i.e. ego, money, possessions. I am ferociously inarticulate about this. I can paint it, because I don't have to search for things. I am in a state of oneness with sky, water, bogland. I am empty, and from that emptiness I receive the painting as a gift.

Polly Devlin
on Ardboe

Writer Polly Devlin revisits her childhood home in Ardboe, County Tyrone, on the shores of Lough Neagh.

I'm sitting on the windowsill of our house in Ardboe. One of the most distinguishing features of this house is the enormous stand of trees about us. Tyrone is traditionally a county of thorn bushes and fairy trees, but these great trees would have been planted by my grandfather around 1911, so they are coming to the end of their lives now. They are full of noisy, chattering rooks, whose sound is so tied up with my childhood. A lot of people would not like rooks about the place, but they are so much part of here that I couldn't imagine this place without them.

We are in the townland of Muinterevlin – 'the country of the Devlins' – in the parish of Ardboe – 'the high cow'. Legend tells of a cow whose magical milk was used in the mortar that bound the stones of the monastery and cross down the road – stones that actually stayed in place for over a millennium. The cow was stolen from the monks but it left the imprint of its hooves on stones as it walked so the monks could track it down. This was given complete credence for us as children when we were shown a stone with a hoofprint down an ancient turf lane.

I grieved when it disappeared but it was later reinstated beside the cross.

There were seven of us. We came in tiers in the space of twelve years – six girls and a boy. It was a paradisiacal place to grow up in, and we were particularly isolated. You look around and you cannot see another house. On one side is the massive natural barrier that is Lough Neagh, while on the other is a great manmade concrete barrier – the aerodrome, built in the 1940s. It effectively cut the parish in half, so that to get out of here you had to take a four-mile-loop around the aerodrome. This was a forbidding and forbidden place to us. We grew up to the sound of Spitfire engines, rather than car engines – of which there were only two, belonging to my father and the priest. The aerodrome, which was inoperable a lot of the time because of mist and fog from the lake, was an extraordinary place, somewhat like a medieval patch of land. When I began to explore it, I developed my passion for natural life. It was a kind of Eden where I sought birds' nests, watched hares bounding across the field, watched the skylark soar and sing from a great height before plummeting to earth again.

It was a paradoxical isolation because there were seven of us who loved each other greatly, our parents, Sarah who minded us, the workers on the land, and then Paddy and Sadie who lived below us and who also had seven children. It is silent now save for the rooks, but imagine the noise and laughter then. This was an independent kingdom of sorts and the absolute king was my father, who wasn't a despot in any way but was so much the central articulation point of the place. I can't imagine what it would have been like to grow up in urban surroundings. Growing up here has left me with a taste for solitude and isolation and a tendency to be almost hermetic at times.

We're on the way to the kitchen now, passing the staircase. Of course, we rarely used the stairs, opting for the banisters and coming to a halt at this lovely mahogany 'egg cup'. Under the stairs was a large metal safe. I can see my father on his knees peering into it and leafing through its contents – mostly share certificates which became worthless after the Wall Street crash. The original red and yellow tiled floor is still here. I use so much of the kitchen detail in my writing – that high shelf with willow-pattern plates ranged along it, for example. In this alcove stood the 'Modern Mistress' – a cast-iron stove that had to be kept up to a red-hot heat and under which the dog would curl up for comfort. And this was Sarah's domain – she was always here, always reliable, always in control.

We move down to the lough. There is the well – a dangerous, magical place in my childhood. I could see my reflection gleaming in the dark water below. Then, to drop a stone into the echoing darkness added to the mystery. Beyond it the beautiful haybarn where.

> ... we found endless diversion, when we jumped dangerously across deep chasms that lay between the teetering stacked bales of straw, when we climbed from beam to beam to look out of the ventilation holes to see the land slipping into the lough, when we played hide

and seek among the corn stacks, when we lay watching the farm cats suckle kittens in the nests they made in high corners of hay out of reach of dogs and foxes, and when we too made nests in the piled-up hay, thirty feet above ground, sinking into its yielding, prickly crispness, so dry it almost burned. (*All of Us There*)

Lough Neagh was a huge dominating influence in all our lives. It is so vast, you could as well be looking out at the Irish Sea. Today the sky is grey, pewter, oppressive, making the lough look like a vast shield of armour, but on other days it can change mood entirely. The slap and the sough of the lough became so much part of us that we didn't hear it. In summer, midges – millions of them – would have visitors choking, but again we never noticed them. And the visitors did come here. It was a tourist attraction even then – to picnic, to swim, and of course to visit the abbey which was (it is said) founded by St Colman. I love to imagine the monks rowing up the lough to arrive at this hill on Ardboe Point, an ideal place to build a church. They were seeking a quiet place with a supply of fish, offering them solitude from the world's temptations and cares. In a way that is how we grew up here too, over a millennium later. The Mass that was celebrated here every year to commemorate the monks was an amazing event.

The priests robe themselves inside the ruined walls and then follow their acolytes out, swinging censers with abandon, so that the fumes of incense envelop us and the subtle and extraordinary noise of open-air prayer begins. The intonations, the declamatory Latin, the murmured responses, the stirrings and rustlings and coughing so pronounced inside the chapel at ordinary Mass, but here drifting quietly upwards to join the cawings of the rooks and seagulls, the hum of the incense-scented midges, all combine to make a far more intoxicating and mystical mingling of atmosphere and noise than any cathedral ceremony. (*All of Us There*)

The lough was of course a working place, like a farm for the local men. They would sit under the bushes on the lee of the Abbey hill and untangle their lines before going out on the water to lay them – often as early as four in the morning. It was their lough, but they were seen as poachers because many years previously the waters had been ceded to the Marquis of Donegal and the fishing rights remained in private hands. The bailiff (his name was King) would patrol in his big motorboat and as soon as he would be seen a warning fire was lit on the shore. King would often lift their lines and tried to harry them out of existence. At the turn of the twentieth century a legal battle over the rights was begun, led by my grandfather, which was finally won sixty years later. The produce – mostly eels – was shipped off to Billingsgate Market in London. We regularly ate eels. From an early age I could skin an eel with my eyes closed, and to do it now it would have to be eyes closed, because I don't subscribe to the killing of fish. I'm a vegetarian.

Here in the graveyard, many of the graves belong to the Devlins. How could you not be affected by that – to see a graveyard filled with people of your own tribe? The high cross is weathered now – there is talk of moving it indoors – but when I was growing up, Frank Quinn from up the road could 'read' each panel. To grow up with a monastic settlement like this was a blessing. We were told that lough water would petrify wood in seven years and in an odd way my childhood has been petrified here, as solid and immovable fact. It was in theory an idyllic childhood but the problem with childhood is that it is so easily made unhappy.

I have wonderful, happy, external memories but I also have internal memories of unhappiness. It was an odd collision. Missing from the graveyard now is the Pin Tree or the Wishing Tree. It was a large tree whose bark was studded with pins, coins and medals. It was essentially used by emigrants leaving for America who left a wish behind. From that a tradition grew that every visitor put a coin in the tree. Of course, the tree eventually died from oxide poisoning. It seemed so immovable and vast to me as a child, like an armadillo with an array of coins for its shell. The trunk should have been preserved. It was a most magical monument with all those wishes and dreams inserted in it.

So many things do remain, however. My life isn't peopled by phantoms but by memory, particularly the memory of my siblings whom I loved dearly and who are all still alive. The fact that we had this rural paradise around us was a bonus. I was moved by reading that Wordsworth said he had been 'sprung' into poetry by hearing a walnut fall.

Wherever we grow up, we have all had the equivalent of Wordsworth's walnut – some secret childhood sound which, if we hear it again, will bring us back to where we were. The walnut in my life came when I was allowed access to the aerodrome and saw the skylark rise from its nest and soar above me. No matter how high it climbs, you never lose sight of it. And then down from this tiny black speck comes this extraordinary song that falls like silvery blue shavings of sound all about you. Anything that is poetic in me was awakened by that sound, the song of the skylark.

In the Footsteps of Jesus

A day like no other when, with a group of pilgrims from Galway, I visited the heart of the old city of Jerusalem, retracing the last days of Jesus on earth, in particular, scenes from his Passion and death.

A 4.30 a.m. alarm call is rarely a welcome sound, but this day would be different. It was Thursday, 20 September 2007, and it was day three of a pilgrimage to the Holy Land under the leadership of our parish priest in Clarinbridge, County Galway, Fr Eamonn Dermody. This was the special day when we would walk in the footsteps of Jesus and retrace scenes from his Passion and death.

We leave our hotel – appropriately named the Bethlehem Inn – at 5 a.m. Across from the hotel the huge thirty-foot wall that encircles Palestinian territory is emblazoned with graffiti:

> Why can't they see that what was done to them they are now doing to us? ... They have the guns but we have the numbers.

Even at this early hour a long queue of Palestinians waits to enter Jerusalem through the heavily-guarded security gate.

We enter the Old City by the Jaffa Gate and assemble to begin the Via Dolorosa – the Way of the Cross. Our group is given a plain wooden cross which we take turns to carry. I am privileged to help carry it at the first and later at the thirteenth station. It is the perfect time to walk the Via Dolorosa through the twisting smelly alleyways. The city hasn't come to life yet. It is quiet, peaceful and cool. We pause for a reading and reflection at each station. Obviously, over the course of two thousand years, for various political and logistical reasons, the Via's route has been changed and reorganised, but that does not matter. We are walking in the footsteps of Jesus. We are carrying on a tradition of great devotion and this is a profoundly moving experience. We are walking with him on his last journey.

I am particularly pleased to be asked to read at the sixth station – Jesus meets Veronica – now located beside a Roman milestone. While there is no mention of Veronica in scripture, I have always loved the notion of the brave, holy woman stepping out from the angry crowd to offer what little solace she could to the condemned man – wiping his face with a towel – for which she was rewarded with the *Vera Icona*, the true image, imprinted on the towel. Her action has always represented true Christianity to me – standing up for Christ when it was anything but easy or popular to do.

The last five stations are within the Basilica of the Holy Sepulchre, where we attend 7 a.m. Mass. Again, mental readjustment is required. Two thousand years ago, Calvary would have been a quarry outside the walls of Jerusalem.

> And they brought him to the place called Golgotha,
> which is the Place of the Skull ... (Mk 15:22)

Now I crawl under the altar of a Greek Orthodox chapel
and reach down through a hole to touch that same
Golgotha. Here his blood and sweat dripped onto this stony
soil. BELIEVE. We move from there downstairs to the
thirteenth station at the Unction Stone and then to the final
station – the tomb of Jesus. We are in touch with the ages.
An overwhelming experience.

After a breakfast of tea and croissants, we visit St Mark's
Syrian Orthodox Church, reputed to be the first Christian
church. We meet a nun, Justina, who sings the Our Father in
Aramaic, the language Jesus would have spoken. Here also is
an icon of the Virgin and Child reputed to have been painted
by St Luke and to which many miracles are attributed.

We exit the city by the Zion Gate to reach Dormition
Abbey, which stands on the traditional site of the house of St
John. A wooden effigy in the crypt marks the place where
Mary 'went into eternal sleep'. Next door is Mount Zion.

> And when they had entered the city, they mounted to
> the Upper Room where were staying Peter and John,
> James and Andrew, Philip and Thomas, Bartholomew
> and Matthew, James the son of Alpheus, Simon the
> Zealot and Jude the brother of James. All these with
> one mind continued steadfastly in prayer with the
> women, and Mary the mother of Jesus, and with his
> brethren. (Acts 1:13–14)

Here truly is the cradle of Christianity, where Jesus celebrated the Last Supper, where he appeared to the apostles twice after the Resurrection, and where the Holy Spirit descended on the apostles at Pentecost. The original Upper Room was probably destroyed when the city itself was levelled in 70 AD, but when the Christian exiles returned, they built a church here which can rightly be called the 'Mother of All Churches'. The very stones seem to speak here. BELIEVE.

On the eastern slope of Mount Zion stands the church of St Peter in Gallicantu, known as the 'Church of the Cock-crow' as it is reputed to be the place where Peter denied Christ.

> 'Did I not see you in the garden with him?' Again Peter denied it and at that moment a cock crowed ... (Jn 18:27)

Here too, Jesus would have spent his last night on earth, imprisoned in a dungeon. Another sacred place. We hear a reading of Psalm 88:

> Lord, why do You reject me?
> Why do You hide Your face?
> Wretched, close to death from my youth
> I have borne Your trials; I am numb.
> Your fury has swept down upon me
> Your terrors have utterly destroyed me.
> They surround me all day like a flood

They assail me all together.
Friend and neighbour You have taken away
My one companion is darkness.

We move outside to the Holy Steps, which linked the old
upper and lower cities and led to the gate near the Pool of
Siloam (where Jesus had restored the blind man's sight and
was castigated by the Jews for doing so on the Sabbath). It
is reckoned that Jesus walked these steps several times in
his last days, as he went to the dungeon, to Gethsemane, to
appear before Caiphas and then to his final trial. Near the
end of a long day of pilgrimage, I am exhausted climbing
these steps. How must He have felt? BELIEVE.

We re-enter the city and pass through another security
check before visiting the Wailing Wall, the remaining wall
of the old Temple of Jerusalem and sacred to the Jews
who come in their thousands to pray and insert petitions in
crevices in the wall.

Day three has ended. There will be other wonderful
days with visits to Bethlehem, Nazareth, the Sea of Galilee,
Mount Tabor, but nothing can equal this extraordinary day
when we literally walked in the footsteps of Jesus in his
final days on earth and every stone and pillar of this historic
city spoke to us about the greatest story ever told. We
return to the Bethlehem Inn, exhausted, humbled, uplifted
and totally overwhelmed.

Catherine McCann
on Shekina

Catherine McCann is a former Sister of Charity, a retired physiotherapist, counsellor and also a writer. In 1979 she bought a cottage with an acre of ground in the scenic valley of Glenmalure, County Wicklow. Over the following twenty years she transformed the garden into the Shekina Sculpture Garden, where by siting individual pieces she could depict the story of creation and provide insight into key moments in our lives. Shekina has thus become a place of reflection and retreat. In 2000, Catherine took me around Shekina.

Shekina is an Old Testament word meaning 'the presence of God', as in the exile of the Israelites when God made known his presence with his people through a pillar of fire by night and a pillar of cloud by day. I felt it apt to name this place thus – a place to find peace, truth, beauty – and maybe God. A feature of the site is a crystal-clear stream running along the perimeter. I diverted it into two ponds at different levels, before it returns to join the Avonbeg River, so no matter where you are in the garden you will hear the music of water. There are eleven formal sculptures, with the garden itself in its contour and design forming the final sculpture.

1. This is the 'The Mystery of Ourselves', a limestone

piece by Fred Conlon. It looks very square from front and back but curvy on the top and both sides. The opening at the centre looks circular from the front but diamond-shaped from the back. Fred's own title for this piece is *Ní mar a shíltear bítear* – things are not what they seem. For me it's about contradictions and the boundaries that shape the way we look at things. We develop the capacity to transcend ourselves and move beyond. We do this by asking questions, so this piece is about arousing questions in ourselves about good and evil in the world and the contradictions we experience within and without us. Each of us needs to reflect not so much on 'who am I?' but 'who I actually am'.

2. 'Absolute Mystery – God.' This is also the work of Fred Conlon, and is a great, strong swirl of granite. He creates a wonderful sense of movement through carving a spiral into a solid piece of Scottish granite. The spiral draws you into its centre and then leads you on into a sense of mystery. For me the solidity and the movement combine to give a sense of the mystery of the Godhead in whom – as Paul said – 'we live and move and have our being'. It provokes an automatic reaction to sit into it and feel secure in its womblike curvature. God is beyond human knowing. As Karl Rahner says, 'God is that blazing reality which is and remains with us Absolute Mystery.'

3. 'Descending Dove' by Ken Thompson. It features the outline of a dove cut out of a piece of stone. It is

the smallest piece in the garden, although it is very effective when viewed from a distance. Ken's idea is that we never see the presence of the Spirit, only its effect is felt. It is through the Spirit that we experience God. Again, this piece links in with the Creation story – 'God's spirit hovered over the water' (Gn 1:2), so I have placed it near the waterfall between the two ponds. Developing the life of the Spirit in our lives flows from keeping in touch with our deep longings, from asking searching questions and from expanding our own loving.

4. 'Creation of the Universe.' This is a set of four magnificent wrought-iron panels by a young metalwork artist, Paul Page. They are seven feet tall and they divide off the garden. They depict the sun, moon, stars, earth, clouds, rainbows, etc., simply reminding us of all the elements that make up our wonderful universe and how we co-create in the ongoing work of creation. Each frame is set in a frieze of celtic design to remind us of our Celtic roots. We are all called to delight in our existence. As Thomas Berry says: 'We cannot live without joy, and that is why I consider life, the universe and the planet earth all as a single multiform celebratory event.'

5. 'Creation of Man and Woman.' This is a marvellous piece of bog-yew, four thousand five hundred years old, sculpted by Michael Casey. It is very much rooted in the earth (Admah/Adam – the word for soil). But we are also upright animals, hence this strong upright

piece carries the sexual symbolism of man and woman together. Michael has written about working on this piece – 'It was on a Christmas Eve that we met. A low winter sun on your form excited me. I sat in awe beside you, you who had existed before Abraham was a boy … at last out of your tangled mess you spoke to me … and I took you into my workshop and we worked together to create order out of chaos … you were no longer a piece of wood but a celebration of life.' I love that last phrase. Our sexuality involves us in becoming givers of life in all sorts of ways. The call to intimacy and to be life-givers is strongly evoked in this sensual piece – people love to stroke it.

6. 'Mother and Child.' This is a fractured bench made from Kilkenny limestone by Noel Scullion. The outlines of a mother and child going to sleep, faces almost touching, are depicted in convex and concave at the fractured ends of the bench. Noel calls it 'Dreamer's Rest'. It prompts me to reflect on the meaning of childhood and, as each of us becomes the maturer child, we are opened to wonder and mystery as we journey on into life's uncharted waters. We must never lose the child within us.

7. 'Lovers.' Imogen Stuart depicts the intimate love that flows between two people in the form of a pair of clasping hands in bronze placed on top of a stone plinth. Some people think they are praying hands, but they are male and female – a strong male upright hand enfolding a smaller curved female hand. For me

it expresses the love of a partnership but also the love between friends – interlocking, yet separate; strength, yet tenderness; equality, yet difference and above all mutuality. I chose two different pieces of writing to help reflect on this theme. One is Martin Buber's idea of an I/Thou relationship; that closeness and space between us as we relate intimately to one another, thus becoming more real. We become more fully human when we are in relationship with others in an intimate way. The other becomes a 'thou' rather than an 'it' to me. The second piece is Margery Williams' wonderful story *The Velveteen Rabbit* – the relationship between a child and a toy helps the toy rabbit achieve a sense of being very real ...

'What is REAL?' asked the Rabbit one day. 'Does it mean having things that buzz inside you and a stick-out handle?'
'Real isn't how you are made,' said the Skin Horse. 'It's a thing that happens to you. When a child loves you for a long, long time, not just to play with, but REALLY loves you, then you become Real.'
'Does it hurt?" asked the Rabbit.
'Sometimes,' said the Skin Horse, for he was always truthful. 'When you are Real you don't mind being hurt.'
'Does it happen all at once, like being wound up,' he asked, 'or bit by bit?'
'It doesn't happen all at once,' said the Skin Horse.

'You *become*. It takes a long time. That's why it doesn't often happen to people who break easily, or have sharp edges, or who have to be carefully kept.'

Significant relationships are so important in our lives – being *real* to and with others.

8. 'Dancers' by Alexander Sokolov features four interlinked dancers. It gives a great sense of joy and connection. We come through life building relationships, and relationships within the wider community are also important. The spaces between the figures are different, suggesting differing relationships within community; each relationship is unique and may require effort on our part. I also focus here on the church as community – first as a pilgrim Church always on the move and so constantly changing, and secondly as a community of sinners (even those who fall badly still belong).

9. 'Death.' We have completed the human story and sadly, or hopefully, our human existence ends in death. This is an important and different piece, since it commemorates a remarkable woman, Marie Webb, who died young, leaving a husband and family. The sculptor Cliodhna Cussen titles this piece 'The Well'. There is an open space on the flat base, which holds rainwater. The round stone at the top symbolises eternity and the cross imprinted on it implies suffering. The piece evokes depth/the unfathomable and in this

instance death. 'I will give water from the well of life; it is the rightful inheritance of the one who proves victorious' (Rv 21:5).

10. 'The Mystery of Jesus' is another piece by Cliodhna Cussen. It may be difficult to see a circular hollowed-out piece of granite sitting on a granite block as the Jesus figure, but I connect it with three statements Jesus made about himself ... 'I am the Resurrection' – bringing us through life and death. 'I am the Way' – the hole in the stone reflects Jesus as the way through life as depicted in the Beatitudes. 'I am the Light of the World.' When Cliodhna broke through the centre opening, she said it transformed the piece, illuminating it by the light that shone through. The piece is untitled, but unsurprisingly it has been nicknamed 'The Polo Mint'.

11. 'Eternal Life.' I was looking for something to symbolise eternity and then I found this piece by the late Alexandra Wejchert – 'Silver Flame' – done in stainless steel. Flame is often used as a symbol of eternal life. The elements play beautifully on it – the slightest breeze brings dynamic life to the 'flames', and the silvery colour catches sunlight most of the day. It's a very beautiful piece.

12. The garden itself is the final 'sculpture' – in its shape, contours, design. The ancient Greeks had the same word for garden and paradise – as symbols of plenty and beauty. When you look up from here, everything – clouds, sky, trees, birds, the sculptures – blends into

a harmonious whole. Nature and man- (and woman-) made pieces blend together to create harmony and beauty. Many people call it a peace garden. We had our first school group here last week and, on leaving, one child made the beautiful remark: 'We loved each other when we were down here.'

Billy Colfer
on the Hook Peninsula

Historian, writer and teacher Billy Colfer explores the unique landscape that shaped him – the Hook Peninsula in County Wexford.

The Hook Peninsula has been part of my life from the day my parents brought me here from London as a newborn. My father came originally from the Hook, while my mother was a native of County Tipperary. It is said that when her father came to visit the newly settled couple, his reaction was 'My poor child, is this where you're living?' The rolling hills of Tipperary were in complete contrast to this exposed, low-lying, treeless and sea-bound finger of land at the mouth of Waterford Harbour. It was an extraordinary place to grow up in. Secluded and also cut off from the rest of County Wexford, there was a very intimately bound community that shared in seasonal tasks – harvesting, threshing, seaweed-collecting, fishing – and in which we as children learned and participated. We also absorbed everything the environment of sea, rock and land offered us, as we roamed through fields and shore.

History is layered all about is. We begin here at the ruin of a medieval church in Churchtown at the top of the peninsula. The church is in turn built on an early Christian site, which signifies the strong connection between this area and Wales. A monk called Dubhán arrived here from Wales in the sixth century and founded a small monastic establishment. From him we get the name for the whole area – *Rinn Dubháin* (the headland of Dubhán) – up to the sixteenth century, when it was anglicised as Hook Head. Dubhán's brother Alloc and his father Brecaun also came here. From the latter, you can see the connection with Brecon Beacons in Wales.

Later in Norman times the Knights Templars acquired all this land and divided it into farms. Subsequently the land belonged to the Redmonds, whose family tomb is in this church. And later still, after the Confederate War in the seventeenth century, the Loftus family of Loftus Hall took over. So there is a whole progression of history in these fields and stones. In their time, the monks of Churchtown became the custodians of the Hook Lighthouse and that will be our next stop.

From medieval times Hook Head has been of immense strategic importance, commanding the entrance to Waterford Harbour, which as *Cumar na dTrí nUisce* (the confluence of three rivers) gave access right into the heart of Ireland. In the epic sixteenth-century poem *The Faerie Queen*, Edmund Spenser acknowledged that, in celebrating the three rivers.

> The first the gentle Súire, that making way
> By sweet Clonmel, adorns rich Waterford;
> The next, the stubborn Nore, whose waters gray
> By fair Kilkenny and Rosporte board.
> The third the goodly Barrow, which doth hoard

Great heaps of salmon in his dreary bosom;
All which long sundered do at last accord
To join in one e'er to the sea they come,
So flowing all from one, all one at last become.

The problem for sailors was the extreme danger that this
low-lying peninsula presented. In the thirteenth century
the Norman baron William Marshall, Lord of Leinster,
established a new town – New Ross – up the estuary from
here, so to mark the extremity of the peninsula he had a
ninety-foot circular tower constructed from local limestone.
It served two purposes. By day it was a landmark that
enabled ships to pick up the tip of the peninsula from
twenty miles out, and at night it had a warning beacon lit
on the summit. It is actually a castle, and only a person
of Marshall's economic standing could have achieved its
construction. And here it is, still solid after eight hundred
years and still working as a lighthouse!

We are now ascending the one hundred and fourteen steps
built into the wall – twelve feet thick at the bottom, tapering
to ten feet at the top. There are two landings on the way to
the top. Here on the second landing you can see the marks
of the planks used in building the barrel-vaulted ceiling. The
lighthouse keepers used to call this room 'the monastery',
because of its intimate connection with the monks, and
those mural alcoves may have been used as sleeping areas
for the monks. Here at the top we have a modern lighthouse
constructed on top of a medieval light tower. We will step
outside. Breathtaking! Literally! This place takes hold of

people. The land is so low-lying, the sky so huge, the sea on three sides, the landscape treeless due to the salt in the air – the whole place has a very atmospheric quality. The prevailing winds blow directly on shore here, especially at Doornogue Point, so if ships were driven onto this shallow rocky area, they were in serious trouble. Over the centuries, hundreds of ships have been wrecked here. Even in my own lifetime, at least twelve vessels have perished. At the top of the Hook you can see the great extent of carboniferous limestone, which has been of huge importance to the area. It has been exploited down the centuries to provide lime mortar for building and lime for improving the soil. There would have been over twenty limekilns around the Hook for burning the limestone and extracting the lime dust. It was a very extensive industry. You can imagine how this building dominated my childhood. It is only when you leave the area that you recall the powerful light flashing in your bedroom window and, on foggy nights, the sonorous boom of the foghorn.

Across from us in a natural inlet on the eastern side of the Hook is the fishing village of Slade, where I grew up and now live, so that will be our next port of call. Before we leave this vantage point, a word about field patterns. Here at the southern end of the peninsula are the large regular fields, owned by the Loftus estate. Around Slade and up to the north are small haphazard fields worked by labourers and fishermen. In fact there are two examples of open fields – large areas in unenclosed strips worked by tenants. One of them, known as 'The Lord's Gardens', comprises twenty acres and is owned by twelve people. So this landscape preserves a medieval landholding in a fossilised form.

Slade is an old English word meaning a valley. It is a tiny fishing port, dominated by a tower-house and hall, which were built in the fifteenth century by the Laffan family. They lost their possessions in the post-Cromwellian period to the Loftus family, who gave the tenancy to William Mansell. He developed the village with cottages, a new pier and a salthouse, the ruin of which still stands. Salt was of huge importance in the Middle Ages. It would have been among the top three imports to this country, being used in the preserving of food and hides. Mansell may even have intended supplying the flourishing fishing industry in Newfoundland (*Talamh an Éisc*), which attracted huge numbers of emigrants from Wexford and Waterford in the eighteenth and nineteenth centuries. Mansell imported rock salt from Cheshire and boiled it here. The salthouse only lasted for his lifetime, as his son let the industry decline. The sea was obviously of huge economic importance to Slade, both for its fishing and its use as a port for boats and small ships. A new pier was built as a Famine relief project but the population declined over the years from over two hundred to maybe a quarter of that number today. At present, ten of the fourteen houses in the village are used as holiday homes.

The other great landmark in the area is Loftus Hall, which is our final stop. The current building, somewhat dilapidated now, is actually quite modern. It was built in 1870 but the site goes back to Norman times. It was previously Redmond Hall (the townland is known as 'the Hall'). The Redmonds came here as tenants of the Knights Templars and became a very influential family before being driven out by Cromwellian forces. It was given to the Loftus family who resided here for more than two centuries. They modernised the estate, improving the land and enclosing the fields. During the Land War there was a turbulent history between tenants and landlord and the ultimate end of landlordism resulted in the sale of Loftus Hall. In 1913 it became a convent and was occupied by the Rosminian Sisters until late in the twentieth century. They converted a room into a chapel, which the locals attended for Sunday Mass. I remember coming to Mass here as a child. Of course the original house's other claim to fame was the ghost said to be attached to it! Anne Tottenham Loftus was reputed to have had an encounter with the devil during a card game in 1760 and became deranged. Strange experiences followed, resulting in the Loftus family inviting the local parish priest to perform an exorcism. He was given two townlands on lease as a reward. The present three-storey Loftus Hall looks gaunt and doesn't fit into the landscape particularly well. Its future looks uncertain.

The Hook is so much part of me and who I am. I grew up in the shadow of Slade Castle and have returned to live here in retirement from teaching. It has a personality and a character all its own. The sea with all its changing moods is about us on three sides. Such is the low-lying nature of the land, the skies above are vast. And dominating this flat, treeless landscape for eight centuries is the wonderful, iconic lighthouse.

The confined nature of the region has produced an intimate, integrated society that has descended from disparate groups of people. Many family names – Colfer included – are deeply rooted here, tracing back to tenantry in medieval times. The Hook is indeed a unique place and very special to me.

On the Edge of the World

A dream was realised when I visited Skellig Rock off the coast of Kerry in September 2000 to make a radio documentary about this extraordinary monastic settlement.

Arrival

Tá mé ag seasamh ar imeall an domhain … I am standing on the edge of the world. So it must have seemed to the men who dared to make this place their home, their place of penitence and prayer almost fifteen hundred years ago. I am standing on *Skellig Mhichíl*, this great fortress standing proudly against the wild Atlantic waves, some eight miles off the southwest coast of Kerry. A wild, unimaginably beautiful place, that for roughly five hundred years was a monastic settlement, the last outpost of Christianity in the then known world. It is a rugged, craggy, barren, dangerous place. It is a sacred place. The stones of the *cillíns* or beehive cells sing out stories of sacrifice and serenity, of deprivation and devotion. It is truly humbling to find oneself a mere human speck on this great rock, which in turn is a mere fleck in the vastness of the Atlantic ocean. I am overwhelmed, fearful almost and totally in awe of this beautiful, wild, sacred place. *Tá mé ag seasamh ar imeall an domhain.*

The Climb

The monastic settlement is some one hundred and eighty metres above me. A long enough climb, but there are some six hundred steps to take me there. What toil went into the cutting of these steps with the most primitive of tools by the men who lived here fifteen centuries ago. I begin the ascent on this mild September morning. The peace is broken only by the call of seabirds, although many of them have by now left for warmer climes. I feel an intruder on their rock, for they truly own this place and even more so the Little Skellig in the distance, whose cliffs glisten like marble thanks to the presence of forty thousand resident gannets – the second-largest gannet colony in the world. Walking along a little ledge, I could fancy I am on the way to heaven! Maybe the monks thought the same when they chose this site.

Two-thirds of the way up I have reached a plateau and contemplate the view. Away to my left is the daunting South Peak, roughly one hundred metres above my level. Up there out on a spit of rock was the hermitage where a monk would do penance and live the solitary life. There, as near as he could be to his God, he prayed and fasted. Now the birds own it, squawking angrily as they soar in and out among the ledges. Rested and refreshed, I tackle the last hundred steps. Even though I could skip one here and there, I prefer to tread every step and walk with the monks. The sea swirls and foams away below me. My laboured breathing betrays my lack of fitness. I step under a stone lintel and take the last few steps under an archway. And here it is – the settlement built by the bare hands of holy men fifteen hundred years ago.

The Settlement

It is, in essence, a village. An engaging cluster of distinctive beehive cells intimately arranged and of varying size and function. Although preservation work is ongoing, the buildings have the appearance of being untouched over the ages. There is the oratory (one of two) where the monks worshipped, the stark cells where they lived, a larger communal cell, the cisterns where they trapped rainwater (the island has no fresh water), the outer terrace that was cultivated as a garden at some period, the stone stairs running down to the sea to landing points from which they faced the Atlantic in their frail coracles. The village still stands in its natural setting, relatively unspoiled. If I close my eyes I can see the cowled figures attending to the mundane tasks of daily life before congregating in the oratory to sing psalms of praise to their God ...

These were men who sought a purer spiritual life in a place apart, and they found it here on this wild rock. They were following a very strong tradition which had travelled across Mediterranean lands to this outpost. Some two hundred years before the monks came here, the first Christian monks sought seclusion in the deserts of Egypt and Sinai – the so-called 'desert fathers'. I clamber into one of the smaller beehive cells. It is perfectly constructed, reasonably dry apart from some damp on the floor, but stark and bare and even on this autumn day, cold. What must it have been like in the depths of winter? I hear the voice of a ninth-century monk ...

Alone in my small cell
Peace for company
Blessed retreat
Before meeting death.
A very cold bed
Fearful
Like the sleep of a doomed man.
Sleep short and restless
Invocations frequent and early
Let this place shelter me
These holy walls
A spot beautiful and sacred
And I there alone.

The first mention of Skellig is in a document written in Tallaght, Dublin, in 798 AD – a martyrology, or calendar of days. On one day there is a mention of 'Suibhne of Sceilg'. About a hundred years later, the Vikings made a number of raids on the island. Little is known about these raids, but the annals do tell us that on one occasion the abbot was taken and starved to death by the Vikings. A small group of ascetic monks persisted here and there was a monastic presence here from the sixth to the twelfth century. They were not hermits, but lived communally, coming together to worship. Perhaps they had a rule of silence apart from prayer – we can only speculate. Then came major societal and Church changes in the twelfth century. The Normans had arrived. Monastic orders such as the Augustinians, Benedictines and Cistercians reorganised the Church. The days of small settlements like Skellig were numbered, and when the Augustinians founded a monastery in Ballinskelligs on the mainland, the monks from Skellig moved there some time in the thirteenth or fourteenth century. Five hundred years of ascetic life had come to an end.

I am now standing inside the church, the second oratory on Skellig. Gazing up at the beautifully corbelled roof, I hear the words of Seamus Heaney as he stood in Gallarus Oratory on the Kerry mainland:

> You can still feel the community pack
> This place: it's like going into a turfstack,
> A core of old dark walled up with stone
> A yard thick. When you're in it alone
> You might have dropped, a reduced creature
> To the heart of the globe. No worshipper
> Would leap up to his God off this floor.
>
> Founded there like heroes in a barrow
> They sought themselves in the eye of their King
> Under the black weight of their own breathing
> And how he smiled on them as out they came
> The sea a censer and the grass a flame.
>
> ('In Gallarus Oratory')

On the way to the terrace garden in the company of Grellan Rourke, conservation architect with the Office of Public Works, my attention is drawn to a tiny building beside one of the cells. It is an architectural rarity – the only beehive

toilet in the country, Grellan assures me. I peer in. Space
for one, sure enough, with a gully beneath where the waste
will run off to the sea. A solitary place indeed. We step
into Cell A, which is substantially larger than the other
cells and has a different orientation. I suggest it might
be the abbot's cell but Grellan thinks it may have been a
communal building, standing as it does opposite the large
oratory. There is evidence of an upper level to which the
monks could ascend. This is obviously a later addition with
more sophisticated features. There are three windows at the
upper level and on the lower level, presses built into the
very deep wall, probably for storing precious possessions.
There are also projecting stones, from which the monks
presumably hung satchels containing prayerbooks. A very
ordered and practical place in absolutely perfect condition
after a thousand years.

We descend a different set of steps on the eastern slope
(there are in fact three different descents to landing places
that the monks used in varied weather conditions). We pass
between two giant pillars that may have supported an oak
door and we are in the Monks' Garden. Looking back to the
monastery, we see an amazing wall with stones several feet
deep. From here it makes the monastery look like a walled
city. Building it was an incredible feat. There is a sheer fall of
hundreds of feet, and Grellan suggests that many may have
died in its construction. The Monks' Garden – protected by
walls that deflect the wind – has in effect its own microclimate.
The monks would have cultivated this garden to provide
much of their food. Grellan and his associates have grown

enormous courgettes here (until the rabbits wiped them out!). The monks almost certainly kept animals here too, and of course fished from the riches of the sea around them. In terms of husbandry, their lives were probably quite similar to the people who lived on the mainland.

Sunset approaches in spectacular fashion. There are splashes of orange, russet and gold on the water. And there is the deep, deep silence, apart from the occasional bird noises. We savour it. It is for me a spiritual experience. What a privilege to be here now in the wake of those holy men. In that silence, the Heaney voice re-echoes across the Atlantic waves:

> The visible sea at a distance from the shore
> Or beyond the anchoring grounds
> Was called the offing.
>
> The emptier it stood, the more compelled
> The eye that scanned it.
> But once you turned your back on it, your back
>
> Was suddenly all eyes like Argus's.
> Then, when you'd look again, the offing felt
> Untrespassed still, and yet somehow vacated
>
> As if a lambent troop that exercised
> On the borders of your vision had withdrawn
> Behind the skyline to manoeuvre and regroup.
>
> ('Squarings, xlvii')

Thanks to the OPW, I am afforded the opportunity of spending a night on Skellig. Another great privilege. The moon is so bright that I can go for a stroll along the base of the rock and savour further the haunting peace and silence of this blessed place.

On day two of my visit, Grellan coaxes me to the South Peak. From medieval times up to the eighteenth century, the South Peak became a place of pilgrimage. Penitents climbed through the Eye of the Needle to the spit of rock, crawled along that before dropping down to a standing stone which they then embraced. I am not *that* brave, but with Grellan's encouragement (and encumbered by a tape recorder and microphone!) I go part of the way, again helped by the monks' quarried steps and even more so by clever little hand-holds that the monks cut into the rock face. There is a sheer drop of one hundred and fifty metres to my left …

With more than a few whispered invocations to the monks for their guidance, I make my way along the ledge – very slowly – until we reach a wider space where we can rest and contemplate what faced the penitents. Again I am in awe at the toil involved in the construction of this Penitents' Way – quarrying the steps and carrying stone and soil all the way to the top. Above the Eye of the Needle I can see little stone walls that created an enclosure for the penitent to trap birds and their eggs. Just to view that climb sends a tremor through my body. It is a real achievement for me to get this far – and hopefully to make my way back down again!

Above: John Quinn, Seamus Heaney and T. K. Whitaker at the launch of *The Curious Mind*, Dublin, 2009

Below: The Coal Quay Market, Cornmarket Street, Cork, c.1900

Above: Tolstoy Love Trees

Below: Bray promenade, Co. Wicklow

Above: A panoramic view of Belfast City, taken from the top of Cave Hill

Right: A disused shipyard in Belfast, Northern Ireland

Below: Ataturk's words on the memorial stone at Anzac Cove, Gallipoli

Above: Daingean Reformatory

Right: Marsh's Library
entrance

Above: Ballyfin House, Co. Laois (Photo: Christina S. Keddie)

Below: Ballyfin, Class of '59 (Author extreme left, third row)

Above: The Western Wall in the old city of Jerusalem

Below: Lough Neagh in Northern Ireland

Shekina Sculpture Garden, Co. Wicklow

Above: Lighthouse at Hook Head

Below: Skellig Michael, off the coast of Co. Kerry

Caftle and Town of Carrick and Abbey of Carrick-beg.

Published as the Act directs by G. Kearsly N.°46 Fleet Street 1 Aug.t 1778.

Carrick-on-Suir 1779 by Paul Sandby

CARRICK-BEG.

Above: Tullynally Castle

Below: High Street, Omagh

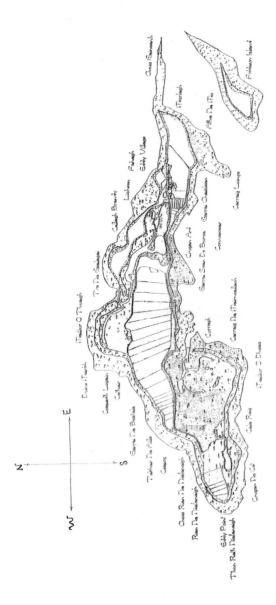

Island Eddy
County Galway

Above: With Anne (left) and Catherine Gregory for the making of the documentary *Two Ladies of Galway* at Coole Park, Co. Galway

Right: The 'autograph tree' at Coole Park, Co. Galway

Above: Toilets in Ephesus

Below: Ancient stone where kings of Ireland were crowned on the Hill of Tara

Above: 'Glendine, Sliabh Bloom' by Thomas P. Joyce

Below: The Auschwitz concentration camp, Oswiecim, Poland

The two islands at Monaincha

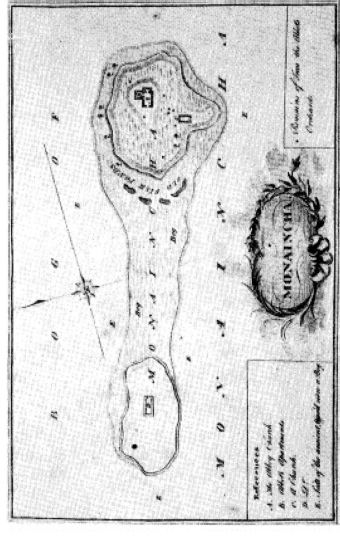

The Ladwich print, c. 1750, shewing the two islands and other features of the ruined abbey.

Above: Monaincha

Below: Dromore school photo 1914

Departure

It is time to leave Skellig. This has been a wonderful experience. Literally full of wonder. It would be impossible to absorb all that this place has to offer in one brief visit, but for now I am satiated. Hopefully I will return. For now I leave Skellig to the gulls, the rabbits and the storied cells. At the conclusion of this indefinable experience I am privileged to return to the mainland in an Irish Lights helicopter. As we lift off, the voice of the poet echoes uncannily in my mind one more time.

> The annals say: when the monks of Clonmacnoise
> Were all at prayers inside the oratory
> A ship appeared above them in the air.
>
> The anchor dragged along behind so deep
> It hooked itself into the altar rails
> And then, as the big hull rocked to a standstill,
>
> A crewman shinned and grappled down the rope
> And struggled to release it. But in vain.
> 'This man can't bear our life here and will drown,'
>
> The abbot said, 'unless we help him.' So
> They did, the freed ship sailed, and the man climbed back
> Out of the marvellous as he had known it.
>
> ('Squarings, viii')

Michael Coady
on Carrick-on-Suir

Poet and writer Michael Coady walks the storied streets of the town where he was born and has lived all of his life: Carrick-on-Suir, County Tipperary.

I am looking down from a hilltop in the lower valley of the River Suir, and in particular at the town of Carrick-on-Suir where I was born and where I live. Technically, I am looking down from County Waterford. Across the river is County Tipperary with the great iconic mountain of Slievenamon to the northwest. To the north is County Kilkenny. I have interacted with this natural hinterland of the town all my life. The river is tidal to this point, and the importance of the tide for navigation between Waterford and Clonmel caused settlement to develop here. The whole Suir Valley was a great corridor to the outer world, a corridor through which invaders came over a thousand years ago. Even long before that we have evidence of people living here five thousand years ago.

In many ways the old central part of the town is a classical Norman creation with the Main Street leading to the Westgate. Below that is the old bridge dating from 1447, the first bridge constructed above the estuary of the Suir. To the east is the Norman castle of the Butlers, the Earls of

Ormond, sited in front of a lovely Elizabethan manor house from about 1560. The Butlers were by and large benign in their overlordship of the southeast. Over three hundred years ago they brought weavers to this town in an attempt to set up an industry here. Carrick became an important town in the mid-eighteenth century, and expanded enormously due to the making and dyeing of woollen cloth. Towards the end of that century, however, the industry declined due to tariffs and the advent of new technology. Subsequently, it never recovered. There are echoes of that in a unique census of the town that was taken in 1799, and to which we will return later.

I am now standing beside the building in which I was born, here on Main Street, at the foot of Cooke Lane. I could locate much of my family history within thirty yards of here, right beside Westgate through which I have passed all my life and a few yards from Oven Lane, where my grandfather was born and where an epic family story began. At the cross above Bridge Street the stocks were located two hundred years ago. We have accounts of malefactors and criminals being whipped smartly from one end of the street to the other, or being locked in the stocks for a day or two. I have always been fascinated by the layers of settlement here, the generations who have lived here through the centuries. I often marched down this street with the local brass band, as my father and uncle did before me.

Like many other Irish towns, Carrick-on-Suir in its modern configuration and its commercial life turned its back to the river. The curve of Main Street exactly replicates the curve of the Suir. We are now turning down one of the many lanes leading to the river – Oven Lane. The word 'lane', in the sense of alleyway, often has painful connotations for Irish people. It is still associated with poverty, squalor and misery in the past and that would be true of the lanes of Carrick – terrible living conditions, high infant mortality, hardship and hunger. That was the case of my ancestors here. The big family story was the death of my great-grandmother in childbirth and her husband subsequently going to America, leaving behind his eight-year-old son, Michael Coady, who became my grandfather. This led me into a deeply layered story. I wrote a poem about it and that led me to making a pilgrimage to Philadelphia to unfold the story. Oven Lane is mostly a car park now, and the poem was a question of the imagination repeopling a place. History tries to tell us what happened, but literature tries to tell us how it felt. I tried to imagine the feelings of the father, a boatman on the river, who had lost a wife and two children. He never said goodbye to the remaining son and never came back. He wrote to his son thirty years later but was never forgiven by him:

> These broken walls were witness
> to your leaving, whether
> in morning sun or rain,
> your firstborn child still sleeping
> when you left him,
> the dark-shawled blessings
> from the doorways of a lane
> you'd never see again.

What I know has come to me
out of dead mouths;
through the barefoot child
left with your father,
the old boatman, and from
the mouth of my own father,
that child's son.

...

Something impelled you,
brought you finally
to bend above
the unmarked page –
an old man

in some room in Philadelphia
reaching for words to bridge
the ocean of his silence,
pleading forgiveness of the child
of Oven Lane.

Silence was the bitter
answer you were given
every empty day
until you died ...

I am very conscious of testament – whether it be the silent
eloquence of the lanes and the buildings or that of the written
record, such as church registers, which are stratifications of

the sacramental chronology of generation after generation. Here in the church sacristy I have spent weeks searching through the registers of baptisms and marriages. I am looking now at my great-grandfather's baptism record on 26 April 1848. The little inscriptions in Latin carry a quality of immediacy in the writing. Revisiting the past with knowledge of what was to come led me to coin the word 'presequence', the opposite of consequence. This was a milestone moment in the life of *Jacobus, filius Jacobi Coady et Margarita Moore*. An offer of one shilling and sixpence was made to the priest – no small amount for a boatman – just a year after the Famine. These registers go back to 1780. They need to be tasted slowly and reflectively. They are a kind of communal lexicon of the story of a people. They convey a compelling sense of absent presence.

We're standing now in the Fair Green. I grew up beside the green but wouldn't have realised then how ancient a space this was. It was the commonage of the town in the twelfth century. I can almost read the history of the last century about me. Behind me is the parish church of St Nicholas and attached to it is the Presentation Convent. The nuns came here in 1813 and gradually colonised almost the entire block. I played hurling in this green in my childhood. This was where circuses and carnivals came and of course where fairs were held. Father Mathew preached on temperance here. Daniel O'Connell held a monster meeting here and the local Temperance Band played 'God Save the Queen' to welcome him. Two hundred years ago the Dorset Militia paraded here. The Dorsets were very popular, unlike the

North Cork Militia who carried out floggings in this space. All of these events find echo now in the empty space of the Fair Green.

I am now standing still only yards from the Main Street, but in a much deeper world. This was what was known in my youth as the Protestant Graveyard. The Heritage Centre behind me was St Nicholas', the last Protestant church, closing in the 1950s. It is adjacent to the Catholic church, so I am looking at a landscape that is a mini-representation of that enormous drama of European history – the Reformation. In the early eighties I came here when this place was an overgrown wilderness. An old friend, local historian Hugh Ryan, and I systematically combed through here, discovering our town's history through its gravestones. I love graveyards – the more overgrown the better! They are very sensuous places that commemorate lives, not deaths. As we cleared and recorded, one of the people I came to know was Little Sally Edmonds. Her stone records that she was born in 1744 and died in 1747, and the mystery of her brief life two hundred and fifty years ago struck me deeply …

> All of human anguish
>   is told upon this stone,
> sorrow's tale is chiselled
>   down to barest bone.

> Did water, fire or fever take
>   this three-year child away?
> Little Sally Edmonds

is two hundred years in clay.
Love that sparked her making
      in darkness of the past
whispered on white pillows
      or smiled in summer grass.

Hairs on head are numbered
      and sparrows count, they say,
little Sally Edmonds
      is two hundred years in clay.

Another stone that I literally stumbled over, collapsed under nettles, commemorated an English soldier, Job Wilks, who drowned in the river in 1868. I am always intrigued by chance and destiny, and it fascinated me to think that it had been Job's destiny to come to our town and die here. It evoked for me the world of Thomas Hardy, as this innocent foot soldier of empire had come from Hardy's West Country:

I feel that I know you Job Wilks –

No imperial trooper swaggering
these servile Tipperary streets
before my grandfather drew breath,
but a country lad out of Hardy,
drunk on payday and pining for Wessex,
flirting with Carrick girls
in fetid laneways after dark
...

On a July day of imperial sun
did your deluged eyes find
vision of Wessex, as Suir water
sang in your brain?

I know the same river you know, Job,
the same sky and hill and stone bridge.
I hope there were Carrick girls with tears
for a country lad out of Hardy
drunk on payday and pining
for Wessex.

We are now in the Heritage Centre, the former Protestant church, and I am looking at an astonishing and unique document – a full census of Carrick-on-Suir, taken in 1799. It is not an official government census, but the work of three remarkable men, primarily William Morton Pitt, an officer with the Dorset Militia. He was an MP with a considerable fortune which he mainly expended on philanthropic schemes in his home county. He was very interested in demography and, with the help of a scholarly local schoolmaster, Patrick Lynch, and an enlightened local merchant, Francis White, he organised a census of this town, aided no doubt by his soldiers in collecting the data. Carrick was a smaller town in 1799 but had double its current population. This remarkable project is a total human anatomy of an Irish town – giving names, occupations, dwelling place, children, other relatives, servants and apprentices. Occasional remarks speak of people being cripples, paupers, idiots. There was multiple

family occupancy – often up to thirty people in one house
with no running water – living in unimaginable conditions,
even though Carrick was considered a prosperous town at
that time.

I drew on this census for my poem 'All Souls', which
describes a memorial journey from the pub to home through
deep November fog, and in which I encounter both the
living and the dead passing through the West Gate with its
clock tower and salmon weathervane.

Orate Fratres (Pray brethren)

for Edmund Kelly the fiddler
and Bartley Lenihan the cockle-carrier
for Mary Cody the baker of Castle Abbey
and Sam Gray the pauper of Pyeman's Lane

for Pat Winton the breeches maker
                and Tim Byrne the weaver
for Ellen Lyons the cider woman
                and John Massey the brazier
for Kate Connors the washerwoman
                and John Brazel the hatter
for Ned Torpey the miller
                and Hannah Connell the huckster
for Brigid Kelly the blind piper
                and Rose Wade the servant
for Jim Haley the brogue-maker
                and Liza Hickey the spinner

for Mary Thompson the cheesemonger
and Isaac Toppin the nailer
for Patrick Lynch the schoolmaster
and Jack Toomey the tailor

A Thiarna an domhain maith dhóibh gach smál
(*O Lord of life forgive all faults*)
Is réitigh leo go flaithiúil fial
(*and show your magnanimity*)
Iad súd a mhair faoi chlog's bradán
(*to all who under bell and salmon*)
'S a ghabh thar bráid an Gheata Thiar
(*passed through the West Gate year by year*)

Finally we come to the old bridge. How many times have I crossed this bridge in my life? I think of all the armies that marched through here, and all the travellers and all the traders. And all the tragedies that happened here. I love to imagine who the masons were who built this bridge around the time of Joan of Arc and the invention of the printing press. This bridge was the scene of possibly the worst river disaster in Irish history. In February 1799 a party of military and their families were travelling on barges from Clonmel to New Ross. The river was in high flood after snow. After a failed attempt at mooring, one barge swung out sideways into the flood and smashed to pieces against the bridge. Over one hundred drowned, mostly women and children, in the space of a couple of minutes. Bodies were found for months afterwards. A plaque commemorates this terrible tragedy, inscribed with lines from an early poem of mine:

> Salmon wait for the tide to still the weir
> Boys are fishing from a bridge
> Built before Columbus raised a sail.

Thomas Pakenham

on Tullynally

Writer and historian Thomas Pakenham reflects on his home and estate at Tullynally Castle, County Westmeath, and in particular on his great passion for trees.

The Pakenhams came here about three hundred and fifty years ago. We came here as carpetbaggers from England in the mid-seventeenth century, enrolling in the army of Charles I to put down the 1641 rebellion. I'm afraid that at various times we changed sides rather nimbly. We joined the Parliamentary Forces obviously at the right time, as we ended with a land grant of several thousand acres here in Westmeath.

The castle is quite large, some three hundred and sixty feet long with many battlements. The house is to some extent a sham because it includes two large courtyards. We are standing in the Great Hall which was originally a courtyard facing the front door, but was covered in in the mid-eighteenth century. What was originally a plain Georgian house grew and grew over the years as the family married and grew richer. The Gothic additions of the nineteenth century have all got ingenious ways of collecting and storing water because there was a scarcity of water to provide for the needs of a large house. Over the centuries each generation of Pakenham has made its mark on Tullynally and its history.

We had one 'black sheep' in the nineteenth century who came to a mysterious end in a hotel in Charing Cross, London, but we have had many eminent soldiers – three generals, one admiral and other lesser ranks. They are commemorated in those fifteen swords you see on the wall before you. The Pakenhams' real break came in 1806 when the younger sister of the then Lord Longford married the man who became one of England's greatest generals and ultimately prime minister – the Duke of Wellington. This, as you can imagine, helped the family fortunes greatly.

How I came to be here is a Little Lord Fauntleroy story. I was leading an innocent childhood in Oxford, where my father was a don, teaching politics and economics. During World War II my sister and I – aged twelve and eleven respectively – were dispatched to Tullynally. It was a difficult time to travel. We came by mailboat to Dublin and from there by taxi to meet my uncle Edward who, together with his wife Christine, ran the Gate Theatre in Dublin. He didn't like me very much but, having no children of his own, I was his heir under a settlement that had been drawn up – so he couldn't really avoid me! That evening we were taken to a pub in Castlepollard by the butler who announced to all present: 'Let me introduce you to the next Earl of Longford!' My sister, who was used to getting everything before me, stepped forward in expectation, but instead it was little Thomas who would inherit the estate. I thought this was wonderful. I always was, and still am, a romantic.

I had read endless adventure stories about the Knights of the Round Table and so on – and now here was this huge castle with its turrets and towers stretching into the mist, all of which would be mine. What could be better? I wasn't thinking then of the problems of heating and maintaining the place. I was, after all, only eleven.

The reality of succession would come sixteen years later with shocking suddenness. My father is ninety-four now [2000] and if his brother was as long-lived, I might be still waiting to inherit the estate. But he died very prematurely at fifty-eight and I found myself precipitated forward to my new role at the comparatively tender age of twenty-seven. I was then a journalist in Fleet Street and I had to say goodbye to that life and become lord of the manor. There were major problems confronting me. I was faced with sixty-two per cent death duties. This is an absurdly large house which to this day has problems with heating and lighting. There was nothing for it but to sell off two-thirds of the assets of the estate to meet the appalling death duties bill. Most people might have said 'call it a day' and get rid of the place entirely but I am a romantic. Anyway, at that time, forty years ago, there weren't rich men buying Anglo-Irish piles as they are doing today. So I stuck it out, and began supplementing my income by becoming a historian, influenced no doubt by my own ancestors' involvement in history.

I like this great hall where we are now. It looks bleak – although John Betjeman once said to me that I should make it even gloomier by accentuating its Gothic character – but six times a year we have two hundred people here, enjoying concerts. The ceiling is two and a half storeys high, so we have wonderful acoustics. The family coat of arms features the motto: *Gloria virtutis umbra* (Glory is the shadow of virtue) and I do my best to uphold it. Also on the wall is an elk-head, dug out of the bog after some twelve thousand years. And here on the floor is this huge, ancient rocking horse, still rocking away, despite the wear and tear of the years. When you think of all the little Pakenhams – myself included – that have sat astride him …

En route to the battlements there is a bedroom that is lined on two sides with books which are very precious to me. They belonged to Christine, Countess of Longford, wife of my uncle Edward. These books were meant to be sold after her death, but I managed to save them. This one by a Chinese travel writer has delightful pictures in the Chinese style of Pakenham Hall, as the house was then known. I also found a sketchbook belonging to my uncle in which he painted the trees on the estate in Chinese style. Only then did I realise how much he loved the trees and he obviously passed that love on to me.

Now on the battlements you will gain an idea of the size of the original estate. It is reduced to fifteen hundred acres now. It extends to Lake Derravaragh, the legendary home of the Children of Lir. You can see a large belt of conifers, which are one of the money-making parts of the estate. We also have a large dairy farm of three hundred cows that helps to keep us going. And there are three hundred acres of wheat, let to a neighbouring farmer under a partnership agreement. Tullynally is an intensively farmed estate. In the distance beside the lake is Knockeyon Hill, seven hundred feet high with an almost sheer drop to the lake. Originally the road went across the top of the hill, but now it goes rather boringly around it so you cannot enjoy the view.

Before we go out to meet some of the trees, I want to show you something here on the terrace. It is a section of a very big old beech tree that blew down on the estate a few years ago. By examining the number of 'rings' in the section we can establish the tree's age, as each 'ring' denotes a year's growth. I can tell you that this tree was planted in 1778. Twenty years later, an outbreak of the 1798 Rebellion happened on that ridge, where the rebels pitched camp, overlooking Wilson's Hospital. So this tree was a silent witness to history. I can also tell when there were years of drought, wherever the 'rings' are narrower, or years of good growth, where the 'rings' are broad. When this tree was about two hundred years old, its neighbours began to fall down, giving it more light and food. So for the last fifteen years of its life the 'rings' are wider. Hence the trees certainly speak to us, telling their own story and also acting as sentinels to history.

Here we are under the canopy of one of my favourite trees – the mighty beech. I look on it as an old friend and I call it Lir, after the king in the Irish legend whose three children were transformed into swans by their wicked stepmother Aoife and banished to nearby Lough Derravaragh for three hundred years. I am always learning new things about this fellow. As the light changes, it creates new patterns almost every second with its foliage. As the seasons change, it is a very different tree. As you can see, it was pollarded about two hundred years ago and five new trunks grew from the pollard points. Then in an extraordinary way they fused together again before arching away once more. Here in the middle of summer, everything seems bursting with vitality and the canopy is complete.

Apart from its architectural beauty, this tree is also a great feat of engineering. It is a structure holding together some thirty tonnes of wood and it is also an engine, pumping water from the ground right to the top of the tree, some eighty feet above us. This is a constantly working mechanism, rising the water in the form of sap through tiny tubes by capillary action. In order to stay alive, every single part of this tree must be covered with a new skin, or bark, which at the extremities of the canopy is microscopically thin. So in those thirty tonnes of wood there are miles of cabling. It is a hugely complicated engineering structure, requiring every single branch to be renewed every year. It draws nutrients up from the soil and then by photosynthesis it turns the sap into sugars and carbohydrates, creating the bark and leaves.

These eleven great oaks are very different from the gnarled old beech. They look elegant and stately. At one hundred and ten feet high, they are the tallest oaks in the Republic of Ireland. There is a saying about the oak – three hundred years growing, three hundred years living, three hundred years dying. An oak can live for up to a thousand years, so at about two hundred and fifty years these fellows are only a quarter of their way through life. It's a salutary reminder to us little humans that they will be here long, long after we are gone!

Postscript (John Quinn)

I returned to Tullynally a couple of years later. As I drove into the estate I immediately sensed something was wrong. King Lir was gone! There it lay already bleached in the summer grass like a warrior felled in battle. Thomas explained that it had been the victim of a violent storm. One of the five great boughs broke off initially, ultimately bringing down the whole tree. Unlike other trees, the five boughs splayed out in different directions, creating the image of a fallen warrior who had died gallantly in battle. Thomas reckoned Lir was about two hundred and fifty years old. What history he had witnessed. It wasn't possible to compute his age accurately as the core was completely rotten. We both grieved for King Lir and later I wrote these lines in his memory.

The Fallen King (for Thomas Pakenham)

Can this be?
This bleached skeleton
Crashed to earth
Amid summer green?
Can this be
The same great beech
'Neath whose massive shade
I stood three years ago
And gazed in awe
Through the dappled crown
That topped its five great trunks?

Lir
You called it
After the legendary king
Who, heartbroken,
Mourned his swan-children
Banished on nearby Derravaragh.

Now this great beech-king
Is also shattered
To its core.
Its five royal trunks
Torn from its heart
Fallen to earth
In stark symmetry.
The fallen king
Now lies in state
On Westmeath earth
A mere swan's flight
From Derravaragh …

Benedict Kiely
on Sweet Omey Town

In 1998 writer Ben Kiely accompanied me on a journey to
the town of Omagh in County Tyrone, where he grew up in
the 1920s and 1930s. It was a journey of memory – we never
left his parlour in Dublin. But that memory is richly peopled
with the characters and events that shaped the master writer
Ben later became. The interview was recorded a few weeks
after the bomb that devastated his town.

Ah! From proud Dungannon to Ballyshannon
And from Cullyhanna to old Ardboe
I've roused and rambled, caroused and gambled
Where songs did thunder and whiskey flow.
It's light and airy I've tramped through Derry
And to Portaferry in the County Down
But with all my raking and undertaking
My heart was aching for sweet Omey town.

That poem stays with me from my childhood days in Omagh.
We called it 'Omey' out of affection for the place, and
probably from the Irish origin. If you were asked '*Cá has tú?*'
(where are you from?) the reply was '*As an Oghmhaigh mé*'
(I'm from Omey). The name meant 'a verdant plain'. I was
actually born in Drumskinny near Dromore on 15 August

1919 – the same date as that of the recent abomination that
devastated our lovely town. My mother was a Gormley
from Claramore along the Fairy Water River about ten
miles from Omagh. She was working in a local hotel when
a gentleman came in one day seriously under the influence.
She promptly gave him a lecture on his behaviour. A week
later he came in again, quite sober, and he proposed to her.
He was my father Thomas Kiely, son of an RIC sergeant
from Bruff in County Limerick. My father joined the British
Army and served in the Boer War, during the entire course
of which, he joked, he never fired a shot except once at a
snake and he never even found out if he hit or missed it!

We moved to Omagh when I was a year old. I have an
early memory of wandering out of the house and then down
the town to the Courthouse, which dominates the sweep of
the town. I saw the vision, as it were, until someone came
and took me home. From the Courthouse you look down
High Street and then you go beyond that to Market Street,
where the awful event happened recently. Then down the
steep hill of Old Castle Street as the great church spires
tower above you.

> The two tall limping Gothic spires rose high above the
> hilly narrow streets. Those two spires and the simple
> plain spire of the Protestant church could be seen for a
> distance of ten miles. They soared, they were prayers
> of a sort over the riverine countryside … Beyond was
> the meeting-place of two rivers, the Camowen and the
> Drumragh – a sparkling trout-water, a sullen pike-

water. United, the waters of Drumragh and Camowen went on under the name of the Strule, sweeping in a great horseshoe around the wide holm below the military barracks, trampling and tossing northwards to meet yet another river, the Fairy Water, then to vanish into a green and blue infinity. (*Down Then by Derry*)

There was a lovely park, a triangular island in the middle of the rivers, called the 'Lovers' Retreat'. The soldiers had another name for it but we won't go into that! The military barracks was a major part of the town. You got used to bands and parades. As secondary schoolboys, we went to the barracks gymnasium for our physical training. Omagh was a great town for bands. As well as the military band, there was St Eugene's Brass and Reed band which my brother-in-law Frank Mc Crory kept going for years. And there were various pipe and flute bands, so we didn't want for music. And we didn't want for ballads or verse either ...

> Thrice happy and blessed were the days of my childhood
> And happy the hours we wandered from school
> By old Mountjoy's forest, or dear native wildwood
> On the green flowery banks of the serpentine Strule.

That's a verse from a nineteenth-century lament for the woodsmen of the Blessington estate in the Strule Valley. There were memories in Omagh of the 'rangers' as the woodsmen were known, assembling in the old potato market – big men, dressed in homespuns, speaking Irish and carrying axes on their shoulders. That verse could also reflect my own memories of a happy childhood. As I said, there were plenty of poets and versifiers around Omagh.

My mother loved to sing and my father was good at recitations, so I grew up in that tradition. There was a postman from the town who emigrated to the US and always wrote home in verse. And there was Andy Mc Loughlin, who was our 'town poet', and indeed was the last town crier of Omagh. He was a charming wee man who wrote ballads about local events and causes – often satirical stuff as good as Pope ever wrote.

> Micky Lynch, you did it dirty. Have you any eyes to see?
> And Alec, what's the matter? You're our Nationalist MP
> McConville and Frank Cassidy, you're not the poor man's friend
> Nor our well-famed bookie, W.F. Townshend.

When a new powerhouse was built in Omagh, the town council gave the job of controller to a Portadown man in preference to a local nationalist. Andy decided to have a go at the town council for this perceived miscarriage of justice. Micky Lynch and Alec Donnelly were members of parliament. McConville, Cassidy and Townshend were prominent businessmen. Townshend had a beautiful daughter, Molly, with whom we young blades all fell in love. The councillors all felt the wrath of Andy.

My brother-in-law, Frank Mc Crory, was a man of music and letters (he was particularly fond of Shaw and Wells) and in his youth was a well-known footballer. He wrote a wonderful comic ballad – 'The Treacherous Waves of Lough Muck' – about two fellows who got lost on the local lake in a snowstorm (or so they said). They actually went drinking in a shebeen until the owner threw them out. Here are a couple of verses:

> People talk of the great Lough Ness monster
> And to see it they come young and old
> But the monsters we saw that wild evenin'
> Leave the Lough Ness boy out in the cold.
> Sharks, sea-lions, whales, alligators
> With mouths that could swallow a truck
> Oh the sights that we saw as we waited for death
> On the treacherous waves of Lough Muck ...

> There we lay on that beach quite exhausted
> Till a man with a big dog drew near.
> He shouted out 'Hi, clear away out of that
> Faith I want no drunk Omey boys here!'
> He said we'd been drinkin' and sleepin'
> Since the clock in his parlour four struck
> And that was the end of our ill-fated cruise
> On the treacherous waves of Lough Muck.

Wonderful stuff, but that is the tradition I grew up in. It was all around me. I had the pleasure of meeting the Rev. Dr Marshall of Sixmilecross, a most gracious and scholarly man who wrote the 'Tyrone Ballads', tales of bachelor farmers in search of a wife, all written in the local dialect.

> I'm livin' in Drumlister
> And I'm gettin' very oul'
> I have to wear an Indian bag
> To save me from the coul'.
> The divil a man in this townlan'
> Wos claner raired nor me
> But I'm livin' in Drumlister
> In clabber to the knee ...

> Me da lived up in Carmin
> An' kep' a sairvant boy;
> His second wife was very sharp,
> He birried her with joy ...

> Consarnin' weemin sure it was
> A constant word of his,
> 'Keep far away from them that's thin
> Their tempers aisy riz' ...

> ('Me an' me Da')

My first appearance on stage at the tender age of nine was to recite 'The Man from God Knows Where' at one of the concerts that were regularly organised in the Town Hall.

I recall shivering with fear in the wings listening to a lady from Derry sing about 'the merry, merry pipes of Pan', before Br Hamill pushed me on stage and I launched into:

> In our townland, on a night of snow
> Rode a man from God knows where ...

I managed to get through the dozen or so verses. In later years I was back on stage in the Omagh Players' production of *The Coming of the Magi*. I actually had a double role, as Annas the high priest and later as one of the Magi. But that was it. Hollywood never came calling!

The aforementioned Br Hamill was J. D. Hamill of the Christian Brothers whose school I attended in Omagh. He was a brother of the great soccer centre-half, Mickey Hamill, which had us even more in awe of him. He had been to China and could never talk of anything but Hong Kong. He would call for me and bring me for walks and was a truly kindly man, but he could never get China out of his system. Then there were two Brothers Burke. T. A. or 'Busty', as we called him, was ex-Blackrock College and a great devotee of rugby, while 'Lanky' Burke from Tipperary was (not surprisingly) a hurling man. Busty had a thing against me – not, God forbid, for anything I did – but because of my brother Gerry who was a staunch GAA man. My good friend Joe Gilroy recounted this to me in later life:

> Your brother Gerry changed Omagh from being a soccer town to a Gaelic football town. We were playing

street football (Gaelic) in Campsie Crescent one day. When you jumped for a high ball, someone hit you from behind and you landed with a bang on the road and hurt your back. A while later we all considered you mad in the head when you went off to be a Jesuit in a novitiate down in County Laois. But the pain came back and your Jesuit days were over! Instead you spent eighteen months in an orthopaedic hospital in Dublin. My point is that if your brother had left Omagh a soccer town, we wouldn't have been playing Gaelic football on the street, you wouldn't have been injured fielding a high ball and you would now be a Jesuit!

He had a point, of course, but anyway 'Busty' Burke had a kind of a 'set' on me. I remember a Br Walker, who was grave and stately but, for a much-maligned order, I found them gentle and good men. Talking of vocations with the Jesuits, I had an earlier 'near miss' with the Christian Brothers. Early on in secondary school, Br McCarthy – 'the recruiting officer' as we called him – gave us a talk and invited us to write an essay about our aspirations for the future. The older students advised us that if we showed interest in the religious life in the future, it might make life easier for us in school. So seventeen of us expressed such an interest. It would mean joining a novitiate in Liverpool, the home of the great Everton footballer Dixie Dean, whose hairstyle – parted down the middle and lathered in brilliantine – many of us imitated. I wrote a particularly flowery essay but in truth it didn't curry much favour with the Brothers and the doubts gradually set in. I explained this on the way home from school to a friend who still saw merit in our decision. 'Even if the worst comes to the worst,' he said, 'we'll get to see Dixie Dean playing every time Everton are at home.' But the promise of Dixie Dean every second week still wasn't enough and neither of us went to Liverpool.

I grew up in a bookish household. My mother would have known Patrick McGill, whose novels were widely read. My brother-in-law Frank Mc Crory had a sizeable library and I had the free run of his books. For some reason I cannot explain, I was drawn to the writings of Chesterton during my secondary school days. This somewhat bemused Frank Mc Crory, who did not at all like the 'Fat Man'. I went with Frank on a late-night excursion train to Dublin for the Eucharistic Congress in 1932. We were in the Phoenix Park at some unearthly hour waiting for Mass when Frank roused me from sleep with the words: 'There's your favourite author carrying the canopy like any respectable Irish publican!' And there indeed was the 'Fat Man', accompanying the Eucharistic procession.

Later in secondary school I was honoured to know that extraordinary Clareman, M. J. Curry, a most respected teacher who influenced all our lives. He would loan his books to us students and ask for our opinions on them. 'And don't just use the books to prop up the window on warm nights!' he warned. I remember too Brother Joyce, with whom we struggled to understand the mysteries of trigonometry. He was also a literary man who would often digress from Maths to speak of and defend the writings of

James Joyce. He made us aware that books were important and indeed that not all writers were dead, as our prescribed texts would have us believe. I was privileged too to meet and become friends with the poetess Alice Milligan, who lived nearby in Mountfield in a smoke-filled house (there were jackdaws in the chimney).

> From the Courthouse steps down the High Street, and up again, and down Market Street, and on the flat and over Campsie Bridge and the Drumragh river, and on the flat again between the tall houses of Campsie, and onto the Swinging Bars ... A gang of us in search of life. Swapping stories, good and bad. Singing, laughing. In search, unwittingly, of life. Practically penniless but mostly content. (*Drink to the Bird*)

And where did we meet? At the cinema, of which the town boasted two fine examples – the Starkinema and Miller's. And at the shops too. Freddy Armstrong's shoemaker's shop was a calling place for grown-up schoolboys. The smoking was wild in there. I didn't smoke myself but you could barely see yourself for smoke in Freddy's. And in my younger days there was Kitty McElhatton's little shop. Kitty made the most delicious toffee apples, which we all craved. She lived past a hundred and died tragically when she took a swig from what she thought was a bottle of stout. It was Jeyes Fluid, a deadly poison.

We had two good newspapers in Omagh – the *Ulster Herald* and the *Tyrone Constitution* – but the best place for immediate news was Davy Young's tobacco and confectionery shop. We would crowd around Davy's window on a Saturday evening to read the football results that Davy posted up for all to see. And not just football results, but the news of the day. I was nine when my brother brought me there to read Davy's notice that Charles Lindbergh had flown across the Atlantic. We all cheered. The secret was that Davy had a wireless set and was happy to share the news with us. He opened the world to us youngsters with his shop window, which was not too far from where that damn bomb went off recently.

There we all were in Omey town. There was no question whether you were Catholic, Protestant, Jew or Presbyterian. We were all neighbours. From my brief career as a sorting clerk in the post office, I recall the music of the local place names – Aghee, Altamuskin, Arvalee, Aughaleague, Augher, Ballynahathy, Beragh, Bomacatall, Brackey, Cavanacaw, Clanabogan, Claramore … where my mother came from. I will always remember Omagh and 'the green flowery banks of the Strule' with great affection.

And when life is over and I shall hover
Above the gates where St Peter stands
And he shall call me for to install me
Among the saints in those golden lands
And I shall answer 'I'm sure tis grand sir
For to play the harp and to wear the crown
But I, being humble, sure I'll never grumble
If Heaven's as charming as sweet Omey town'.

Katie Martyn
on Island Eddy

Katie Martyn is a friend and neighbour of mine in South Galway. She was born and reared on Island Eddy off the coast of Galway. This is her story of that life, recalled to me in a journey of memory in 2015.

The Island

Island Eddy is a small island off the coast of South Galway. The nearest village in the mainland would be Ballinderreen. I was born on the island in September 1927, the seventh of eight children born to Patrick Bermingham and Kate McDonagh. There were seven families on the island then although I am told there were fourteen families living there before our time. There were three Bermingham families, two Keanes and two Conlons. The three Berminghams were originally my grandfather and his two brothers who married two widows whose husbands had died in a boating accident. They were coming from Galway when an animal put its foot through the boat and it sank.

Each family had seven acres of the best of land walled in and they had access to commonage beyond that. Each house also had a half-acre allotment (the *coinicéar*) for early potatoes. We also had a 'cabbage garden' for vegetables at the gable end of the house. The land was tilled right into the wall for barley, wheat, oats, turnips and mangolds. There was neither briar nor bush. I never saw a blackberry until I came to the mainland. There was one horse and one cow per family, a few sheep, a plough and harrow and maybe a roller. Mangolds were chopped with a scythe affixed to a piece of wood, and turnips were crushed with a stone.

The island was owned by the Redingtons of Kilcornan who were good landlords. There was a photograph of one of them in our house. As a child I always thought he was our uncle. Our family were the only children on the island in my childhood. The Keanes later had children but they then moved to Kinvara.

My father and my uncle Mike used to sail over to Connemara each summer to buy turf. Mike never married but lived with us. He was a great help to my father with the farming and harvesting seaweed. In 1917 my father met Kate McDonagh in Carraroe and they married the following year. She would have been a native Irish speaker and my father had good Irish too but they never spoke Irish to their children. I think they felt that speaking Irish made them second-class citizens. They only spoke Irish to each other when they had something private to discuss.

In the space of eleven years eight children came along – Tom, Nora, Willie, Marty, Mary, Winifred, myself and Pat – but sadly Winifred died suddenly at three weeks. It may have been a cot death. She was buried in the *cillín*, the children's graveyard on the island. Originally there was just a big stone to mark it, but a few years ago we put a proper headstone there, otherwise no one would know where it was when

Pat and I are gone. There is one adult buried in the *cillín* – a military man whose body was washed ashore. My father married late in life so I never knew my grandparents. I was baptised a couple of days after my birth in my home by Fr Michael Walsh from Ballinderreen, who came out by boat. I suppose it would be too dangerous to bring a newborn to the mainland. Although it was a new life for my mother, she loved the island. She worked very hard, became a widow at a young age and it pained her to see her children emigrate one after another. There was no other way, but at least we all got a good basic education. My earliest memory is of running along beside her as she carried Pat in her arms and took food to the workmen in the fields. It was summer and I was barefoot and of course all the summers seemed beautiful then!

The houses were more or less built to the same design although, as I remember, some had no back door. There were three bedrooms and a kitchen. The big bedroom doubled as a 'parlour' – I remember a glass case and fold-up table and chairs. The bed would be screened off for the 'stations', when the priest came to say Mass and hear Confessions. This happened twice a year – in May and October – and was especially for old people who couldn't get to Ballinderreen. The stations would rotate through the houses and when our turn came the whitewash and the paint would be out to make everything look spick and span! The priest would also collect dues on both occasions, and he brought a supply of *Sacred Heart Messengers* for people to read. There would be a full breakfast laid on for him. The neighbours would have tea and bread or cake before dispersing for work.

The younger people went to Mass in Ballinderreen. A few times a year at low tide there would be a *trá* (dry strand) when you could walk the mile or so to Aran Pier, but otherwise six or seven of us would take the punt. If the weather was rough we would go to Rihairne, walk by a *cosán* (pathway) to Aran in our wellies, then put on our Sunday shoes and walk the couple of miles to Ballinderreen. We would leave at nine o'clock to be on time for eleven o'clock Mass. On the way back we would call in to Mrs Kelly's shop at Aran Hill and she would have the tea ready. She was such a kind lady. She ran a general store and it was a busy place. The men who had a pint or two in Ballinderreen would then join us for the return journey. Often we would go shopping on a Saturday and I would do chores for Mrs Kelly – sweep the floor or fill bags of tea, sugar or bread soda. She would have a lovely currant cake as a treat for me. If we bought bran or pollard or paraffin oil, Mr Kelly would deliver it to Aran Pier and then the women would row the punt back. If there was a big shop to be done – for sacks of flour for example – we would take the sailboat to Kinvara. The post for the island was delivered to John Tierney's house on the mainland and he would keep it for us.

I loved Christmas. Each house would have a big red candle in the window. When you looked over at the windows in Ballinacourty, it was like a small town. My mother would raise twenty or thirty turkeys and sell them to Mr Pigott from Gort. The turkeys would have their legs tied and wings crossed when we brought them live to Aran Pier where Mr Pigott collected them. My brothers would dredge for oysters in December and sell them to Linnane's or Moran's at one pound per hundred. It was extra income for Christmas. We children didn't get anything fancy from Santa – just a stocking with fruit, sweets and little trinkets. The boys might get cap guns. I was going to school a while before I got my first doll. We always had goose for Christmas dinner. We raised our own geese, hens, ducks and pigs. We would kill three pigs a year. The bacon would later be hung on a crook in the chimney to 'smoke' it. A lamb was always killed for the feast of St Martin (11 November). We ground our own corn and made wholemeal bread. We caught mackerel and herrings. Mother would gut them and put the mackerel out to dry on a big rock. They were like kippers. The herrings were salted and kept in a barrel. It was a very varied diet, you could say.

There was no fresh water on the island. We collected rainwater in a tank that was cleaned twice a year, so we never got sick from it! If the summer was very dry we would go to Clarinbridge with four or five barrels in the boat. There was an amazing freshwater well near the shore on Keane's farm. Some of the women might go to help fill the barrels with buckets and maybe do some shopping in Clarinbridge. Then when the tide came in, they sailed for home. A horse and cart would be waiting with an empty barrel. You filled that barrel (using a bucket) and then repeated the process with the remaining barrels. It was hard work.

There was no school on the island in my time. There had been a tiny school there in my father's time. It was little more than a shed. I went to school in Maree on the mainland because I could stay with our second cousins Michael and Mary Agnes Athy. They had no children so we were a sort of ready-made family for them. My brother Willie was nearly finished school when I started at age seven at Easter 1935. You couldn't go to school until you could look after yourself properly – wash, dress, tie your shoes and so on. I had been taught a lot at home by my big sister, Nora. I knew my prayers and could write, so I went into first class straight away. The teacher, Mrs Riordan, was very kind and gentle. She was like a mother to us, but I was very lonely at first, knowing I wouldn't be back on the island until the holidays came. On a Sunday we might go down to Ballinacourty and when you looked over at the island you would be kind of heartbroken but gradually you grew reconciled to the situation. Our mother would visit too. We would be very excited, watching out for her.

I would do little jobs for Michael – bring in the cows for milking in the morning, have breakfast while they were being milked, drive them back out and then off to school. Michael had another, bigger farm two miles away in Rinville, so he was regularly moving sheep or cattle over and back. When that happened I would be kept home for a day or two to drive the animals and stand in gaps! I had to rely on my friends to catch up on my lessons each time. When it came to Pat's turn, he didn't like the idea of school at first, because as the youngest he had a great time, being the only child on the island. We had much shorter summer holidays than now – from late July (just before the Galway Races) to early September. It was lovely to enjoy the freedom of home

– running, skipping, splashing in the sea at our front door, building sandcastles with shells and broken china – doing the normal things that children love to do. I only remember one big storm when the sea came right up to the front door. It was very frightening, looking out at a wild sea. Pat and I thought we might have to climb up to the loft where mother kept the spinning wheel, but luckily the water never came into the house.

I was brought home from school when I was fourteen because my father was dying. Dr Tubridy from Oranmore (she would be related to Ryan Tubridy of the *Late Late Show*) said he had cancer and had only a week or two to live, which proved correct. He was waked at home for a couple of nights, while the sailboat went to Kinvara for a coffin and food and drink for the wake. People who had connections with the island came over for the wake and then the sailboat set off with the coffin and family, followed by a procession of punts. It was a very sad journey. Then on the mainland the coffin was brought to Ballinderreen church and finally to Drumacoo cemetery in a hearse drawn by two black horses. People said they heard the *bean-sí* crying but it was more likely the cry of the seal at Fidín.

There was a good social life on the island. Nora Conlon and Winnie Keane played the melodeon and we had a gramophone to provide music for dancing, which was very popular. If anyone came in at all there would be a dance – half-sets, the Siege of Ennis, the Walls of Limerick. Card playing was also very popular on winter nights, as was storytelling. You would skip home very quickly after hearing a few ghost stories. People also read a lot of books, although you might only get a newspaper on a Sunday. In 1947 the Conlons got a radio (money from America) and you can imagine how popular that was! It had a dry and a wet battery and every so often the wet battery would be brought in a special box on the bus to Galway to be charged. There would also be occasional visits to Galway on the sailboat to a *feis* or to buy paint or limestone. In summertime three hooker-loads of turf came from Connemara to provide winter fuel for heating and cooking. The light came from paraffin lamps and later the tilley lamps, which were much brighter.

I went with my sister to Carraroe for a holiday once and my uncle Jimmy brought me on a trip to the Aran Islands, where he was delivering turf. A big storm forced the other boats back but Jimmy kept going. We were drenched and stayed a night on the island before returning to Carraroe. It was quite an experience! There were no tragedies on Island Eddy in my time, but we were told about a teenage girl who walked across the strand to get horseshoe nails for her father. Unfortunately she was caught by the tide on her return and drowned.

I remember a big treat in 1939 when Michael Athy brought me to Dublin to see Galway play hurling. We even went to Bray to see Nora who was working in a hotel there. Galway lost, but what a thrill it was to spend a whole weekend in the big city! The islanders all got on well together. We helped each other at work – cutting corn with the scythe and hand-binding the sheaves. There would be a lot of laughter, especially when the sweet can full of tea and the cake were produced. We were like one big family really, visiting each other regularly. The front door was always open. And there was no crime! The guards came now and then to check gun and dog licences. Every family had a dog, but we hid them when the guards came! What harm could the dogs do anyway? The guns were for shooting wild geese and ducks – and the crows that were a nuisance when the corn was planted. There were no rabbits on the island.

I finished school in seventh class at fifteen years of age, but I stayed on with the Athys as Mary Agnes became ill and died quite young. I stayed a few years at home until at the age of twenty I joined my sisters to work in London. My mother wouldn't dream of me going until then – she was afraid I would get lost! London was amazing, even though in 1948 it still bore the scars of war. We had to make our way through bomb sites to the shops and rationing was in force – four ounces of meat and two ounces of tea a week. We certainly missed our Island Eddy food, that's for sure! And on my first day in London we travelled on the underground and I saw a black man in real life for the first time! It was a real culture shock, even more so in the wire factory where I worked. Initially my cockney instructor Doreen and Island Eddy Cathy (as they called me) failed totally to understand each other! Gradually things improved, however.

I later got a job in a plastics factory nearer our flat. I was punching out up to twenty-five thousand patterns a day on a kind of sewing-machine but never found it boring. I earned three pounds, ten shillings a week. We spent a lot of time and money going to the pictures and to dances on Saturday nights. I loved London and was never lonely, although the fact that five of my family were working there helped. On Sunday afternoons I would write home and slip in a ten-shilling note when I could. My mother would reply with the one letter that we all shared.

I didn't come home for two years and when I did in 1950, the plan was to return after Christmas. On my first Sunday home John Martyn came on the scene and that was the end of the plan! We married in the following April. I was the last bride from Island Eddy. I came across to Ballinderreen in my wedding costume and we had the wedding party in John's home. The barn was cleared out and seating was put in. John's sisters did the catering – legs of mutton, turkey (supplied by my mother) a ham, tomatoes, and jelly and custard! The party went on till six in the morning while we slipped away to Kilcolgan to catch the bus to Limerick for a few days' honeymoon. We were subsequently blessed with six children – four girls and two boys.

My mother left Island Eddy in 1955 and lived in Galway until she died in 1976. It makes me lonely now, even to see the island in the distance. I was so happy there as a child and a teenager. It was the people, the fun, the laughter. I last visited it about forty years ago. I stayed a couple of nights with Mary Bermingham. She was one of the last to leave the island permanently. Nearly all the houses were derelict. It broke my heart to see them. I cried and cried with loneliness for what had been. I vowed never to go back again and I never have. It was too much to bear.

Anne and Catherine Gregory
on Coole Park

Having read Anne Gregory's delightful memoir of her childhood at Coole Park, County Galway – *Me & Nu* – I invited Anne and her sister Catherine (Nu), now in their eighties, to come back to Coole and share their memories of growing up there, under the care of their extraordinary grandmother, Lady Augusta Gregory.

We are here at the walled flower garden and there's the tree we climbed as children. It was higher than the wall, so we could look in and see what Tim Gormley was doing in the vineries. There was a sort of boilerhouse behind the vineries where Tim would eat his lunch. Sometimes we would nip up and steal his lunch – the most delicious soda bread you ever tasted! And never once did he complain.

As we enter the garden you can see the remains of one of the two great catalpa trees that grew here. There is a photograph of Grandma sitting under one of them but that tree has gone. When Sean O'Casey came to visit, Grandma explained that many years ago one of the Gregory ancestors had brought these trees with him from his tour abroad – ten feet tall and rolled up in cloth – and had planted them here in Coole. O'Casey was fascinated by this. When he came here he knew absolutely nothing about trees but Grandma gave him lessons on how to identify trees – the beech, the fir tree, the plane tree – and he became really passionate about trees from then on.

There was an orchard here in the garden and huge ilex trees and a tennis court, but the most famous tree of all was the beautiful copper beech, which became known as the 'autograph tree'. Grandma would invite her guests to carve their initials on this tree and you can still see most of them nearly a hundred years later. We actually watched O'Casey carve his name and he did it so well, we asked him why? He told us he was used to carving his initials on the desks at school. Augustus John climbed to the top of the tree to carve his initials but Grandma made him do it again here at the bottom. There it is – along with George Bernard Shaw, John Masefield, Douglas Hyde, Jack Yeats, W. B. Yeats, Violet Martin (who was Catherine's godmother), Sally Allgood and John Quinn, Grandma's American friend. So if *this* John Quinn is going to sign it, you had better put John Quinn, *Junior*!

We are now in the nut wood. We would meet Mr Yeats a lot down here. He wasn't really interested in children but he wasn't in any way rude. He would say 'hello' and move on, humming his poetry aloud. Of course you must remember that as children we had no idea that Grandma's visitors were very important people. To us they were just adults (often boring adults!) who happened to be Grandma's friends. Mr Yeats did tell us once that he came across a badger here in the nut wood, which allowed him to stroke his head! Of course if it had been a real badger, it would still be holding

Mr Yeats' hand! It was our little dog, Taddy, which had a head like a badger. We loved to come down here on our pony, Pud, and donkey, Tommy, and try to act out *Swiss Family Robinson*, our favourite book that Grandma read to us. We would build tree houses, hunt with bows and arrows (though we never actually killed anything) and try to convince Pud and Tommy that they were really a zebra and an ostrich.

We are standing now in front of where the house (Coole Park) once stood. The kitchen and larders were in the basement. There was a square porch with the hall door at the side of it. On the right-hand side when you entered there was a cloakroom and then what we called the 'tiny dining room', which led into the pantry. You went from there down steps to the kitchen at basement level. On the left-hand side there was a breakfast room with a bathroom and a small bedroom, which was originally the gunroom. Upstairs there was our playroom, which was huge, and Mum's bedroom with a dressing room and bathroom off it. Then there was the drawing room, a lovely big room with portraits on the wall. It was here that Grandma did her writing at a desk in front of the window. And then there was the library, lined from ceiling to floor all round with beautiful, leather-bound books. It was more of a sitting room really, a family room where on winter evenings we sat in front of a roaring log fire and Grandma read to us. We loved the library.

We always had an enormous Christmas tree, even if we were on our own. Grandma would mark a tree early in the year as the one we were going to have, and it was kept specially free from grass and ivy so that it wouldn't grow lopsided. It was always put up in the breakfast room late on Christmas Eve, and Grandma and Mamma decorated it after lunch on Christmas Day. We weren't allowed to see it, either before or after it was decorated, until we were called in – wild with excitement – when all the candles were alight. The room looked like fairyland with the silver star glittering at the tip-top of the enormous tree, nearly touching the ceiling; the candles flickering made all the pictures on the walls appear to move with the light coming and going on the glass; the masses of piled parcels at the base of the tree, and masses more little parcels in bright paper tied on the branches among the fairylike decorations; and above all, the wonderful, heady smell of hot candle-grease. (*Me & Nu*)

The only building still standing here in Coole is the stables, now the visitor centre. There was hay and timber stored there and of course the horses were stabled there, especially Sarsfield, our father's favourite. Across from the stables a whole array of carriages and coaches were housed – the Victoria, the brougham, the wagonette, sidecars, traps – and there was a harness room in the middle. Beyond the wall was an immense manure heap, under which they have since discovered marvellous spring water. We have suggested that they market it as Coole Water! There was also a forge that had what seemed like millions of bats – I can still smell them!

This is the kitchen garden, but we knew it as the apple garden. It was here that we would stock up with apples for our trips into the woods. The best way to carry them was to put them in our knickers – we wore those long navy-blue knickers, elasticated at the knee. We could carry up to a dozen apples each, but it meant that we couldn't walk properly! One day we bumped into our mother and Augustus John, who were out walking. There was a look of horror on her face.

'What on earth is wrong with you children? Have you had an accident?'

'No Mamma,' we explained, 'It's the apples …'

'Apples? What apples?' We showed her. She was totally disgusted and made us take all the apples out at the knees of our knickers. Augustus John was falling about the place with laughter but Mamma was not at all amused.

(The rain eventually forces us to take refuge in the visitor centre restaurant where, over tea and buns, Anne and Catherine reflect on the extraordinary influence their beloved grandmother had on their lives).

Grandma was the centre of our lives here in Coole, where we were born and bred. She wasn't just Grandma – she was really our mother. She could be quite a disciplinarian, but for her the important things were 'always be on time' and 'manners maketh man'. She had incredible friendliness. Class or creed meant nothing to her. If in the middle of a day's work, someone came to the door looking for apples or sticks, it didn't matter to her. She would come down and have a chat. The extraordinary thing was while we were having this wonderful life here, she was writing, running the Abbey, going up and down to Dublin and over to London to fight for the Lane pictures – but she would always have time for us. She might be in the middle of writing a play when we would rush in to tell her of a bird's nest we had found. She would drop everything at once to hear our story.

She was our teacher – and a slightly easy-going one too. She taught us our tables and simple arithmetic, some French also, but her pronunciation was appalling. We had to read a chapter of the Bible to her every morning. She would read to us every evening, anything from Brer Rabbit to James Fenimore Cooper. *Swiss Family Robinson* was our favourite book.

When you look at photographs of Grandma, she looks like Queen Victoria – all in black – but she actually had a great sense of humour. She was never a prude. We had a general knowledge book full of questions like, 'Why in public places does water at drinking troughs always come out of the mouth of a lion?' Grandma said, 'Well, it would look awful coming out the other end!' and then exploded into laughter. She just couldn't stop. I can still see her with her hankie up to her eyes, the tears streaming down her cheeks.

She also made us learn poetry by heart, although – strangely – never any poems by Mr Yeats. He was the worst reader of his own stuff – like a bad clergyman with an artificial 'pulpit' voice. When he wasn't writing, he would

go around humming to himself. Grandma said that was why
his poetry was so good to recite aloud – because Mr Yeats
used to hum it to get a rhythm on it before he wrote it. He
wasn't interested in children – why should he be? We were
just children. His son Michael used to tell how Mr Yeats
didn't recognise him when they passed on the stairs once!

When I (Anne) was somewhat older, Mr Yeats sent for
me one evening and read me a poem he had written about
my hair:

> Never shall a young man
> Thrown into despair
> By those great honey-coloured
> Ramparts at your ear
> Love you for yourself alone
> And not your yellow hair ...
>
> But I can get a hair dye
> And set such colour there
> Brown or black or carrot
> That young men in despair
> Shall love me for myself alone
> And not my yellow hair.
>
> ('For Anne Gregory')

I was very embarrassed. I thought it was awful but of course
I said, 'Read it again.' Soon afterwards he read it on a radio
broadcast. Next morning there was a letter for me from my
then boyfriend. It said:

If I was alone on an island
And only Anne with me there
I'd make myself cushions and bolsters
By stuffing her skin with her hair!

That was the end of that romance!

Of all the visitors to Coole, GBS (George Bernard Shaw) was our favourite. He was a natural with children. Mind you, he was always cheating. During the Great War we couldn't have jam *and* butter on our bread. It had to be one or the other. GBS held up a dry slice of bread and asked for jam, but we had seen him butter the other side. We were horrified – and of course raging that we hadn't thought of his trick. We also found him peeping through his fingers when we played 'Hunt the Thimble'! It was so embarrassing to see a grown-up cheating and we said this to Grandma. She was very hurt and told us we must send some of his favourite apples to him in London to make up. We did that and then got this marvellous poem from him, written on five postcards:

Two ladies of Galway called Catherine and Anna
Whom some call Acushla and some call Alanna
On finding the gate of the front garden undone
Stole Grandmama's apples and sent them to London ...

And Grandmama said that the poor village
schoolchildren
Were better behaved than the well-brought-up Coole
children

And threatened them with the most merciless whippings
If ever again they laid hands on her pippins …

When Grandma died, we were desolate. It was like the end
of the world to us. Coole had always been our home, even
though we were grown up by then. We never felt we needed
anything but what we had, which was the woods and our
ponies and Grandma. It was a perfect life.

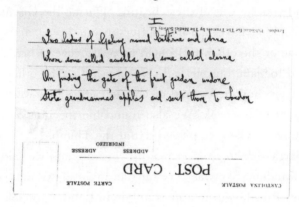

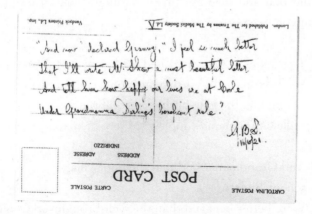

Above: Postcards from George Bernard Shaw containing a poem for
Anne and Catherine Gregory

Ephesus

In 2014 an opportunity arose for me to walk in the footsteps of St Paul, down the marble streets of Ephesus …

Ephesus. There is a ring of antiquity about the name. A place once glorious but now lost. And indeed it was once glorious – a seaport on the western coast of Turkey, once the capital of Asia Minor sustaining a population of a quarter of a million, the gateway to the great trade route to Asia. Once, but no more. Once the venue for a great Council of the Church in 431 AD (a year before Patrick came to Ireland). Once the home of the missionary St Paul, before he was banished and subsequently wrote letters of support to the Ephesians who had earlier listened to his preaching. These latter facts represented the sum total of my awareness of Ephesus before I arrived at its gates as part of a tour group on a misty November morning in 2014.

Once a seaport? But we had travelled inland for an hour from Kusadasi on the Aegean coast to get to Ephesus. And now the sea was no longer even visible. Some explanation is necessary. Ephesus was originally established at the mouth of the Cayster River on the coast, but serious earth movements – mainly alluvial deposits from the river – caused the town to be relocated not once but four times. The site we are visiting today is in fact Ephesus number three – or rather the 20 per cent of number three that has been uncovered so far. But as we are to discover – what a 20 per cent!

Partly, I suppose because of its strategic location, Ephesus has had a troubled history. At various stages it was ruled by Persians, Greeks, Goths and Romans. Its glory days came when Alexander the Great captured the city in 334 BC and on Alexander's death, one of his generals, Lysimachos, became the ruler and moved the city to the valley between Mount Koressos and Mount Pion. It is this Ephesus that we are exploring today.

We walk between two rows of columns nearly two hundred metres long. This is the *basilica*, where in Roman times merchants traded and bankers changed money. On one side is the *odeum*, a small theatre with tiered seating for fifteen hundred people. Here the rich Ephesians and the *curetes* – priests who dealt with religious and state affairs – would discuss the city's problems and here also concerts were performed. On the other side of the basilica is the *agora*, the great assembly place for public meetings. In one short stroll we have been at the centre of the governing and business life of Roman Ephesus.

Gradually it is the ingenuity of the Roman town planners and builders that begins to amaze us. Here is the ruin of the Water Palace, one of the largest buildings in the city, which stored the water requirements of Ephesus. Now our footsteps echo down the Curetes Street, so called because the bases of the columns at the entrance to this street were inscribed with the names of the *curetes*. Statues of famous

Ephesians were placed in front of the various stores on both sides of the street. It is tempting to close your eyes and imagine the noisy bustle of this street in its heyday. Chariots and carts trundle over the uneven marble flags. Voices call out. I hear too the slap of sandals on the flags. Paul and his band of disciples on their way to preach their message to a not always welcoming crowd ... Later, in exile, he would continue to write to the Ephesians. His words were probably conveyed to the crowd by his disciple, Timothy.

> Bear with one another charitably, in complete selflessness, gentleness and patience. Do all you can to preserve the unity of the Spirit by the peace that binds you together. There is one Body, one Spirit ... There is one Lord, one faith, one baptism and one God, who is Father of all, through all and within all. Each one of us, however, has been given his own share of grace, given as Christ allotted it ... to some, his gift was that they should be apostles; to some, prophets; to some, evangelists; to some, pastors and teachers; so that the saints together make a unity in the work of service, building up the body of Christ. (Ephesians 4)

We come next to the Scholastikia Baths, another triumph of Roman design and engineering. There is a *frigidarium*, or cold room, a lukewarm room and ultimately a *caldarium* or hot room, where the water was heated by hot air circulating through brick columns. There is marble everywhere. Other parts of the baths offered a resting room, libraries and gymnasia. The baths, which could serve up to a thousand people, were thus two millennia ahead of our modern spa/leisure centres. Just beyond the baths is a building that intrigues the modern travellers – the public latrines. A large U-shaped building that could serve up to fifty people at a time. Practicality obviously overruled dignity with the Romans. They sat side by side in public, did their business and moved on. A water-channel beneath connected with the sewer that ran under the Curetes Street. And a water-channel in front provided ablutions for the latrine users. Oh, those clever Romans!

Across the street from the baths, a number of houses are being excavated and restored. These houses, usually two-storeyed, would have been the homes of rich Ephesians. The walls are decorated with magnificent frescoes and floors and ceilings feature symbolic mosaics. At the bottom of the Curetes Street we come to one of the treasures of Ephesus – the Celsus Library – named after a second-century Roman governor. This magnificent two-storey building, although burned and ruined by the Goths in the third century, has been partially restored in recent times, with the statues at the front symbolising the wisdom and knowledge of Celsus. This building is thought to have stored some twelve thousand roll books before its destruction. In front of the library there is a space where philosophers gave lectures. Did Paul speak here, I wonder? From the Celsus Library we proceed along the magnificent Marble Road – a thing of great beauty that survives from the period of Greek rule. There is even a pathway on either side for the safety of pedestrians and again a sewage system underneath. This road leads us to the most impressive Grand Theatre – a huge amphitheatre originally built by the Greeks and later enlarged by the Romans to seat twenty-five thousand people. What dramas must have been played out on this stage! Here also the Romans protested against the teachings of Paul, as Christianity began to take root in Ephesus.

Another wide marble street – Arcadian Street – ran straight to the original harbour where visiting rulers landed and travelled in pomp into the city. Over the centuries, deposits of alluvial mud caused the sea to retreat some five kilometres, and by the end of the first millennium Ephesus was no longer an important port or trade centre and it had shrunk from a once glorious city of trade, learning and elegance, to little more than an obscure village. For me, however, visiting its ruins two millennia after its heyday was an awesome experience. To marvel at its marble streets, its beautiful library, its Grand Theatre and the ingenious design and engineering work of the Romans (water palaces, aqueducts, baths, sewers and, yes, public latrines!) was a memorable experience. Subsequent visits to Pergamon and Troy would also fascinate me, but nothing on this tour would speak to me like the marble streets and great monuments of Ephesus.

And all the time I thought of Paul, once the persecutor of Christians and now their teacher and advisor. As I looked down the Arcadian Road to where the port was in Paul's time, I promised myself that on my return home I would seek out that moving account of his departure from Ephesus in Chapter 20 of the Acts of the Apostles ...

Paul addressed these words to the elders of the church of Ephesus: Be on your guard and for all the flock of which the Holy Spirit has made you the overseers, to feed the Church of God which he bought with his own blood. I know quite well that when I have gone fierce wolves will invade you and will have no mercy on the flock. Even from your own ranks there will be men coming forward with a travesty of truth on their lips to induce the disciples to follow them. So be on your guard, remembering how night and day for three years I never failed to keep you right, shedding tears over each one of you. And now I commend you to God, and to the word of his grace that has power to build you up and to give your inheritance among all the sanctified. I have never asked anyone for money or clothes; you know for yourselves that the work I did earned enough to meet my needs and those of my companions. I did this to show you that this is how we must exert ourselves to support the weak, remembering the words of the Lord Jesus, who himself said, 'There is more happiness in giving than receiving'.

When he had finished speaking he knelt down with them all and prayed. By now they were all in tears; they put their arms around Paul's neck and kissed him. What saddened them most was his saying they would never see his face again. Then they escorted him to the ship.

Michael Slavin
on the Hill of Tara

In 1998, Michael Slavin accompanied me on a walk across the Hill of Tara, County Meath, the ancient seat of the kings of Ireland. Michael has lived at Tara for most of his adult life and is the author of the definitive guidebook *The Book of Tara*.

I love this place. I always had a fascination for Tara as the heart of Ireland. In my youth I was away from Ireland for about twenty years. On my return I had no definite abode in mind. I was drawn to this place and I haven't left it since. That was thirty years ago.

This is a sacred place for me. Our ancestors came to the Boyne Valley about seven thousand years ago. Tara is the highest hill for miles around and is only four miles from the elbow of the Boyne where settlement took place. A number of streams flow from here to the Boyne so the settlers would have been attracted to it, associating it with the Earth Mother Goddess who provided a rich harvest for the winter. In time Tara became a coronation place for kings and ultimately the Royal Palace – a living place for kings.

It is a big site – one hundred acres – which is now owned by the state. Prior to that, the owners had the right to charge sixpence to enter the site. One owner in the nineteenth century was an English prime minister, Lord

John Russell, who inherited the hill as part of his estates in 1839.

We are heading across a field, near the entrance to the *Teach Míodhchuarta* or, as it is popularly known, the banqueting hall. It resembles a huge trench seven hundred feet long, with a bank on either side. The *Book of Leinster* describes the banqueting hall as having one hundred and fifty sections, with fifty warriors in each, for the great festival that was held every three years in Tara. It is nice to speculate that this indeed was the location of the banqueting hall, but some recent historians suggest that this was a ceremonial entrance to Tara. Personally, I like to think that there was possibly a standing stone at the end of this *cursus* and at a certain time of year the shadow cast by the stone would run right down the *cursus*, thus indicating the starting time of the festival. We simply don't know. The early people of say five thousand years ago looked on the world in a very different way to us. I'm not ruling out the possibility of this being the banqueting hall – or even a succession of halls. If it was, what a spectacular scene it must have been when such an assembly took place. Remember, the legends also tell of the five great roads that radiated from here across the country. Imagine the bustle and clamour along those roads at festival time!

As we make our way to Rath Gráinne on the *grianán*, the sunny western side of the hill, the view from here is impressive. It is said that points in sixteen counties can be seen from here – the Wicklow Mountains to the south, round the Hill of Allen in Kildare, where the Fianna had their camp, across the whole Central Plain to the Shannon and then north to Sliabh Gullion and the Mournes. One of the names given to this place was Teamhair, the 'place of great prospect', ultimately corrupted to Tara. We are now at Rath Gráinne, a great circular mound associated with the legendary Gráinne who was betrothed to Fionn MacCumhaill, leader of the Fianna. She considered him too old and eloped from here with Diarmaid. Thus began the legendary pursuit of the pair across the country before Diarmaid died on Ben Bulben and Gráinne returned here. Tara's history is layered. Although this *rath* has never been excavated, there is evidence that it was built over previous mounds. The top of this mound is saucer-shaped, suggesting there might be a burial chamber underneath.

Just across from Rath Gráinne are the two sloping trenches. Again, there are legends associated with them. One is said to have slipped down the hill when a king pronounced a wrong judgement. The other is said to have been the scene of a mass slaughter of maidens when Dunlaing, King of Leinster, invaded this place in 222 AD. Below us to the west there is a beautiful grove of trees – for me one of the most beautiful places on earth. On a warm, sunny day like today I like to wander in under the great sycamores to find little sheltered spaces where I can sit and rest and be at peace.

I should mention how central the sun was to the lives of the ancient people. The rising of the sun was recorded at various times – *Imbolc*, the budding time of the year, *Bealtaine* or Maytime, *Lughnasa* or August and *Samhain*, the great end of year festival. Likewise the full moon acted as a kind of calendar. The mighty sun was associated with the heavens, with powers beyond the people. It was the ancients' clock, their image of what controlled the fruitfulness of the earth and what made things happen. When a king was inaugurated here, it was done with the concept that he would intervene between his people and those powers that they didn't understand. He was, as it were, wedded to the Earth Mother Goddess and, if accepted by her, he would be a king who would ensure rich harvests in season.

On our way back up the hill we pass the fairy tree – a lone hawthorn bush that visitors respect for its other-world connections. It is festooned with medallions, ribbons, beads that people from all over the world have affixed to it. We come then to the Rath of the Synods, deriving its name from synods or meetings of bishops and abbots that are said to have taken place here in Christian times, when Tara's importance was beginning to decline. Early in the twentieth century a strange thing happened here. A group of devout Israelites came here, convinced that the Ark of the Covenant was buried in this mound – and they were allowed to dig for it! They found nothing but some Roman coins. Later, in the 1950s, an official excavation revealed post-holes that suggested substantial wooden buildings in former times, as well as Roman artefacts that suggested commerce between Tara and the continent.

One of the reasons I wrote *The Book of Tara* was that I seemed to be forever reading accounts of Tara that began: 'Tara is a disappointment ...' They asked: 'What is Tara but a hill with a few mounds?' I didn't like that. This is a place of history, of power, of mystery and lore stretching over thousands of years. Tara is, to a degree, what you make it yourself. *Dúchas*, the heritage service, have put an interpretive centre in the old church here to help us understand the place. I just hope these mounds will be maintained to the highest degree possible, so that people will experience this beautiful piece of lush Irish countryside. This is a precious jewel that has survived undisturbed and unchanged for thousands of years. Let's hope it will be just as beautiful a thousand years from now.

We have now come to the outer rampart of the central ceremonial area of Tara – *Rath na Rí* or the Rath of the Kings. This comprises sixteen acres and, viewed from above, it is the view most people would associate with Tara – two intersecting mounds making a figure of eight. The more westerly mound is the *Forradh* or the King's Seat, where judgements would have been made in the round wattle and thatch house that sat atop it. Again there is evidence of previous mounds under the *Forradh*. The layers of history once more. Legend has it that one of those older mounds holds the grave of a Spanish princess of the Milesians, Tea, who wanted to be buried on 'the fairest hill in Ireland'. And so we get another derivation of the name Tara: *Tea-Mhuir* or the Wall of Tea.

The second mound in this space is known as Cormac's House, a reference to one of Tara's greatest kings, Cormac Mac Airt, who reigned in the third century and was associated with the great warrior Fionn Mac Cumhaill and his army, the Fianna. History and legend are interwoven here, so we have to be careful, but Cormac's reign has been described as 'a golden age of plenty' and a tenth-century poem tells us that 'when Cormac was in Tara, a kingly equal of his was not be found in all the world'. This whole Rath na Rí area is very impressive, about a mile in circumference. The outer ring is quite daunting. The builders dug eleven feet down into the rock – probably heating it with fires and then pouring water on it to make it split. They then built it up as a ramp about six feet wide, with probably a palisade inside that. It had specific funnel-shaped entrances to make this a reserved area. This would have been the White House of its day. I like to imagine visitors being welcomed here from abroad and at certain times a great fair in progress with athletes and entertainers performing and debates being held. This place is so emotive of power. Imagine a king looking across the Central Plain, thinking of the thousands of cows he could have there, for cows were a symbol of wealth and a medium of exchange. Little wonder that the King of Tara eventually became the King of Ireland.

There are also more recent layers of history here. When Daniel O'Connell set out on his campaign to repeal the Act of Union, he chose significant historic locations for his 'monster meetings' – places like Clontarf and this Hill of Tara. He convened a meeting here for 15 August 1843 and it is said that over half a million people answered his call. What a sight it must have been – people streaming here on foot, others in carriages or carts, with bands playing to welcome O'Connell as he arrived in cavalcade from Dunshaughlin. A contemporary report on his long speech said that 'his words flowed down the hill like honey'.

Almost fifty years earlier, this hill was the scene of part of the 1798 Rebellion. Some four thousand 'croppies' or rebels assembled here but they were poorly organised and were mowed down by the local yeomanry. Many of the croppies were buried here and the ancient *Lia Fáil* or Stone of Destiny was moved from its previous location to mark the croppies' grave. In 1948 a Celtic Cross was also put here to commemorate the '98 rebels. The *Lia Fáil* was said to be the coronation stone for the kings of Tara. Legend has it that the ancient people, the *Dé Danann*, brought three gifts to Tara – the other two were the Sword of Light and the Cauldron of Plenty. We may scoff at the idea that the *Lia Fáil* would emit a roar when touched by the rightful king, but for the ancients the stone incorporated the spirits of their ancestors. Myth and legend! What can we say? What do we know?

We come to the final and oldest mound – the Mound of the Hostages. Its story goes back some five thousand years and it was excavated in the 1950s by the great archaeologist Seán Ó Ríordáin. There is an interior chamber some fifteen feet long. On the left is the beautiful engraved Stone of Tara with its life-force image of concentric circles with smaller images of the moon and stars. Who knows what these images signified for the people who carved this stone thousands of years ago? Ó Ríordáin found evidence of over two hundred cremated human remains in little cists along the chamber. He also found the skeleton of a teenage boy with precious stones around his neck. A young prince? A boy king? The mystery continues. The mound gets its name from the practice of an overking demanding hostages to keep lesser tribes under control. These hostages would not have been slaves, but important people who were treated by the overking as if they were in their own home. One such king of Tara was Niall of the Nine Hostages from whom descended the O'Neill dynasty that ruled Tara from the fifth to the eleventh century AD. This mound was a place of ritual and of burial – a very sacred place.

Our walk concludes at the nineteenth-century Church of Ireland building that was deconsecrated in 1991 and is now an interpretive centre that features a beautiful Evie Hone stained-glass window of the Holy Spirit. It is the third church on this site, reaching back to Norman times. This is where the Celtic and Christian worlds met. In the churchyard and inside the church are ancient carved stones from the Celtic era. They remind us of yet another legend of Tara. Candidates for the kingship had to drive their chariots towards two sacred stones standing closely together. The stones would only move apart for the rightful king!

How could you not be bemused and entranced by a place of such legend! Personally, I just feel wrapped around by a place that I love, by its nature, its history, its legends and, walking this sacred hill, I always feel a deep sense of touching the soul of Ireland.

Here once stood the royal seat
Silent now but not forlorn

For this is still the Ard-Rí's home
Cernait, Gráinne, Cormac, Fionn
'Twas here they loved and lost and won
Their secrets beneath Tara's soil
Known only to the Lia Fáil.

('A Song of Tara')

Tom Joyce
on the Slieve Bloom Mountains

In 1995, artist and sculptor Tom Joyce accompanied me on a day-long walk through parts of the Slieve Bloom Mountains in County Laois. He had just published *Bladhma – Walks of Discovery in Slieve Bloom*.

We are in Glenbarrow, near the village of Rosenalis in County Laois, on the northeast side of the Slieve Bloom mountains. It is a place that became my home and completely changed my philosophy of life when I came to live here in 1981. As the name implies, we are in the valley of the Barrow River and we are watching it tumble down from its source, about three miles from here. It is hard to imagine that this is Ireland's second-largest river, as we observe it here. It has no distinct well source, but it creeps out from under the blanket bog above us and begins as an innocent little trickle. Here in Glenbarrow, with the help of the rain beating down on us (in the middle of June!), it has become a raging torrent as it leaves the valley. In winter it will rise by another three feet. I can hear it then from my home, thundering and echoing down the valley. I have witnessed whole trees being washed down by its awesome power and have heard rocks rumble along its bed. It can be a frightening but very spectacular sight to view it from the security of this vantage point, ten feet above the water.

The very rocks we stand on are part of a sandstone pavement some three hundred and eighty million years old, which puts our story into a timescale. The dinosaurs died out one hundred and sixty million years ago. Mankind came on the scene less than two million years ago. The cliff of debris across from us was deposited by Ice Age glaciers fifteen thousand years ago. All of these time-points have lots of noughts in them – most of us will be lucky to have one nought! It gives a sense of mortality to watch this river rushing below us, slowly grinding rock into sand and gravel that will be recycled long after we are gone. We have a short time-span as humans and in appreciating that fact we realise we are not the pinnacle of creation, but just another part of the jigsaw. Just like the mountains worn down by the river's passage, our time will reach its zenith and then fade away. So this place doesn't just speak to me – it screams at me!

We have now moved around the bend in the river to the Clamphole waterfall, formed by the overhanging sandstone rock collapsing into the river. It is quite a spectacular sight – you can see an entire beech tree lodged in the plunge pool. I have a memory of coming up here after two days and nights of heavy winter rain. The river was huge, seething, powerful, clawing at its banks with an alarming ferocity, its spume filling the air. Whole trees washed past me. So it is a place that lends itself to myth and legend. Fionn Mac Cumhaill is said to have lived here. Those enormous sandstone flags are like a giant staircase – fitting for a giant like Fionn? The origin of the name Bladhma (Bloom) is shrouded in mystery. It is possibly derived from a mythological figure but nothing is certain. I like that mystery, that uncertainty.

When I first came here, I knew the names of very few plants. I knew nothing of geology and had but a passing interest in archaeology. Through living here, exploring the place, I have developed a deep interest in those things, which has added to the quality of my life. That is what Slieve Bloom offers to me – a wonderful quality of life. A wet, misty day like today only adds to the magic and mystery of the place. I regard it as a female entity – a beautiful woman who has captured my heart and continues to seduce me! History is here. In the shallower water below us are little ripples in the sandstone – similar to those seen in the sand at the seaside. They formed in the channel of a river that flowed here about three hundred and eighty million years ago. Undisturbed and covered by finer deposits, they became fossilised. Charm is here. Beauty is here. Apart from being my home place, my whole philosophy of life is grounded here, as are my appreciation of the aesthetic and my artistic development. This is where my inspiration comes from.

The waterfall may be the more spectacular attraction of Slieve Bloom, but there are many other little places of beauty and spectacle. We have now come around to the western end of Slieve Bloom and we are standing in a field beside a large stone slab which is known as Fiddler's Rock. It is a great block of quartzite, deposited here by a glacier some twelve thousand years ago. It is in direct alignment with a Bronze Age tumulus – a passage grave similar to Newgrange in County Meath – about a kilometre away to the north.

If you drew a line from here to the tumulus, it would pass between and at right angles to two weathered pillars of limestone about seven feet apart, so there is a definite system of alignment here. When I became interested in this place, I found evidence of human settlement. Right behind Fiddler's Rock there is a circular earth bank, probably a ring fort. Behind it on Cumber Hill and Knocknaman, there are two hill forts. We are at the meeting of three townlands – Forelacka, Cumber and Glenafelly. The great *Slí Dála* (the road to Munster), one of the five great roads from Tara two thousand years ago, passed through here – right past Fiddler's Rock, which would have been a kind of waymark or signpost. A branch road through Climber Valley would have led to the monastic settlement of Seir Kieran. Heading north through Knocknaman would have been the route to the northern part of the country. So we had a kind of crossroads here, which would have led to settlement, and ultimately quite a populated area, here in this remote part of Slieve Bloom.

Story and history are all about us. In his introduction to my book *Bladhma*, the environmentalist John Feehan writes:

> Every detail of the ground is a relic of human endeavour; things on each walk reflect the human influence at every level, extending in time from the present back to the human beginning. The pine stumps on Knockanastumpa are all that remain of woods in which the first farmers hunted …

This is true of every landscape. If you keep peeling back the layers, like the pages of a book, you get deeper and deeper into the story.

We have made a slight detour on our travels, especially for you, John. Here on the eastern fringe of Slieve Bloom is Ballyfin, originally the great stately home of the Coote family, but for the past seventy years it has been a boarding school run by the Patrician Brothers and I understand you spent five memorable years here in the 1950s, John! It is one of the five great houses of Slieve Bloom (Roundwood, Derry, Summergrove and Cardtown being the others). It is part of the heritage of Slieve Bloom and it needs attention because it is literally withering away. The sandstone is weathering badly. As we move through the magnificent entrance salon, through the rotunda and into the splendid library, we can only marvel at the wonderful ceilings, floors and fireplaces. But then here in the 'gold room' we see the beautiful cornice seriously damaged by rain leaking from the roof. It is very sad to see this beautiful house under threat, so if there is a kind millionaire listening to this programme, perhaps he could throw a few millions down this way.*

We have now come to a very different landscape. This is a place called Srahan. We are sheltering under a whitethorn bush, looking down through a canyon of furze. This is a special place for me. A sad place. It is a *cillín*, where unbaptised infants were buried. They weren't considered as

---

* How prescient Tom Joyce was! A few years later that is what happened! For the full story read 'Ballyfin' elsewhere in his book.

qualified to be buried in consecrated ground. Those little upright marker stones are the gravestones of these children. This site was chosen because it was a sacred site. Folklore has it that this was once a monastic settlement. There is also a large slab of Galway granite deposited here during the Ice Age. Such stones had special significance for Bronze-Age people. There is a great sense of loss and tragedy here. To the passer-by it might seem just another 'bit of a field' but again, peel back the layers. The last burial here was in the 1930s – infant twins who died at birth. I have often sat under this tree and thought long and hard about life and death. For me it is not a morbid place but peaceful, calm – and tragic. I get the same sense here as I have got at World War I cemeteries I have visited – utter peace and calm.

We are now in Baunreagh, right in the heart of Slieve Bloom, standing on a beautifully constructed bridge over a culvert. This was an eighteenth-century toll-road that crossed the mountains northward from Mountrath. Further down the hill is a little spring well, protected by a lovely sandstone wall. The crystal-clear water flows through a channel carved in the sandstone flags. This is possibly where horses would stop to drink before undertaking the big climb northward. Baunreagh is closely associated with William Stuart Trench who lived at Cardtown House, about three kilometres from here. He set about the reclamation of Baunreagh Valley which had been a largely heather-covered area. In the mid-nineteenth century he employed a technique of cutting back the heather, ploughing it back into the ground and then mounding the soil and heather in 'lazy beds', fertilising them with *guano* (bird manure imported from South America). We can still see the pattern of the lazy beds, about one and a half metres wide. The land improved so much that corn was also grown here. Trench employed about two hundred labourers and the area became known as the 'Happy Valley' for its prosperity.

Trench was awarded silver and gold medals by the Royal Agricultural Society for his pioneering work, but unfortunately it all ended in tragedy. In 1846, Trench planted one hundred and sixty-two acres of potatoes. Further down the lowlands, there were rumours of a new disease – potato blight. Trench rode down there, saw its effects, smelled it and knew the devastation it caused. He checked his own crop in Baunreagh on 1 and 2 August. All was well. On 6 August as he rode into the valley, he recalls in his own account (*Realities of Irish Life*) how he could smell the potatoes rotting in the ground. There was nothing he could do. 'Happy Valley' was no more.

Just a bit further on from Baunreagh is an interesting hawthorn ditch. I learned from an old neighbour, Mick Dunne, how it had been spaced and layered. A straw rope was made, the haws were inserted in it and the rope was then soaked in a mixture of urine and rainwater. The rope was rolled up, a trench was dug and the rope was buried in it. The urine duly rotted the straw, turning it into compost that fertilised the seedlings. It was the pattern of this ditch in Baunreagh that made me curious as to how such ditches were created. Human ingenuity!

This is Knocknastumpa – a bleak and desolate bogland. This open moorland is probably what Slieve Bloom in its entirety looked like seventy years ago, before huge tracts of forest were planted. You can see the evidence of turf banks where people from my own valley – Glenbarrow – cut turf over the years. The turf was then drawn by horse and sleigh across the heather. The special thing about here is that as the bog was cut away it exposed a pale grey gravel left here by the ice. On top of that gravel are the tree stumps of the ancient pine forest that covered Slieve Bloom four to six thousand years ago. Again, peeling back the layers ... This turf-bank is four feet deep, representing four thousand years. One inch of that bogland represents our human lifespan. We have become so arrogant, seeing ourselves as the pinnacle of evolution. We should realise we have only a short time as a life, never mind as a species. Similarly, these mountains were once as high as the Alps. Now their maximum height is one thousand seven hundred and fifty feet. Three thousand metres of limestone have been eroded through the ages. To put it another way, if you sit in a room with a standard eight-foot ceiling, the time we humans have been in existence as a species is the equivalent of one hair's breadth, whereas the height of the room represents the length of time life has been on this earth. Oh, we're an arrogant bunch alright!

We conclude our Slieve Bloom ramble in a cemetery – the Quaker burial ground in Rosenalis. A lovely, peaceful place, beautifully kept. I love the sense of order here, with all the gravestones in lines orientated north to south, no elaborate monuments or Celtic crosses. All the same and simple – grey limestone with black inscriptions. No ostentation. That is the way it should be. And yet it is a very spiritual place.

Our ramble today has been about how Slieve Bloom has moved my spirit and affected me. I cannot traverse these mountains without being deeply moved. For me, this is an appropriate place to end.

> Ye who love the haunts of nature,
> Love the sunshine of the meadow,
> Love the shadow of the forest,
> Love the wind among the branches,
> And the rain shower and the snow storm
> And the rushing of great rivers
> Through their palisades of pine trees,
> And the thunder on the mountains
> Whose innumerable echoes
> Flap like eagles in their eyries –
> Listen to these wild traditions …

(From H.W. Longfellow, 'The Song of Hiawatha')

Into the Darkness

30 September 2004. Day three of a group tour of Poland. We have enjoyed a visit to Chopin's birthplace in Warsaw; the fantastic experience of the Wieliczka Salt Mine – an underground world of labyrinths, lakes and a wedding chapel carved out of salt; the beautiful city of Cracow with its magnificent churches and its old market square. Days of light and beauty. But today is a descent into darkness. We are visiting Auschwitz.

The very mention of the word pierces the heart with jagged-edged blades – coldness, savagery, extreme suffering. AUSCHWITZ. You have seen the films, studied the photographs, read the accounts, heard the stories. But nothing can prepare you for the impact of the electrified barbed wire fence that encloses this huge site, the stark brick barracks, the gas chamber and crematorium. Nothing.

Auschwitz-Birkenau National Museum was established in 1947 as a monument to the terror and extermination that over a million people suffered here in its five-year existence from 1940 to 1945. When the Nazis abandoned the camp in January 1945, they tried to eradicate the evidence of what had happened there by demolishing many of the buildings, but enough remains to tell the true story of Auschwitz. Every year millions of people come here to be reminded of that story and on this grey September morning our coach is one of many arriving in the huge car and coach park, disgorging groups of many nationalities who have come to undergo the Auschwitz experience – in my case with some trepidation and not a little unease.

The Auschwitz camp had a dual purpose – as a concentration camp for prisoners of various nationalities, mainly Poles, and later and more horrifically as a centre for the extermination of Jews. In the space of three years somewhere between 1.1 and 1.5 million Jews were murdered here. The whole project was based on a lie. Trains arrived here from all over Europe with deported Jews who assumed they were heading for a better life. Even if the 'trains' were little more than cattle wagons, the grainy film footage of their journeys depict the sense of adventure on the faces of many of the Jews, particularly the children. For a lot of them this would have been their first journey on a train.

On arrival at the camp the lie continued. Gardens were landscaped to delude the somewhat bewildered arrivals, to ensure there would be no panic. But when they stepped out on the dreaded ramp it was decision time. The SS doctors and guards decided who would live and work and – in the case of mothers, young children, the old and infirm – who would die by gassing. The final lie lay in the metal inscription over the main entrance – *Arbeit Macht Frei* (Work Will Set You Free). For all but a tiny minority, freedom would never be a reality. Even for those fortunate enough to be working, malnutrition and starvation ultimately led to their deaths too.

We follow our guide along the brick barracks, block after block, each of which housed hundreds in the most basic conditions – triple-tiered wooden slatted bunks with the most primitive sanitary and washing facilities. Block 10 was the scene of the most inhuman sterilisation projects on Jewish women. Block 11 was notorious for its punishment cells, including the standing-only cells. In one of these blocks, Joseph Mengele carried out his horrific experiments on twins. If one twin died he had the other one killed, to compare post-mortems ... Here too is Maximilian Kolbe's cell, where the priest took the place of a condemned prisoner. Between the two blocks is the Death Wall where prisoners were shot – strangely reminiscent of the wall in Kilmainham Jail. And all the time I ask myself: Why? Why? Why?

We enter a remaining gas chamber – the 'shower-room'. A shudder goes through me as we are shown original ZYKLON B canisters from which the poisonous granules were poured through the ceiling ... There were five gas chambers/crematoria in Auschwitz and a further four in Auschwitz 2 or Birkenau as it is known. These buildings were capable of killing and disposing of twelve thousand Jews a day. We move into the remaining crematorium. To touch the incineration oven is a surreal experience. I can only fall silent and remember and pray. In 1944 the extermination was so intense that the crematoria could not cope and the bodies were burned in pits. Horror upon horror upon horror.

At one time there were some thirty sheds that housed the paltry belongings of the prisoners – suitcases, clothes, shoes.

Today in the exhibition hall there are huge display cases stacked high with suitcases, shoes, spectacles, women's hair and, poignantly, children's shoes. This is simply two hours of heartbreak for today's visitors. What must it have been like for the original inmates, however brief or long their stay? Endless suffering. No hope. Hell. We are brought to a cinema to view that experience in a series of harrowing films. It is almost too much to bear but I feel I owe it to those suffering people at the very least to be aware and to remember.

We travel the few miles to Birkenau. Although there is less to see here – most of the buildings have been demolished – it is the sheer vastness of the place that is terrifying. The site stretches almost as far as the eye can see. Again, the cramped sleeping conditions and the horrific sanitary facilities are on display. How they must have suffered, especially in the bitter Polish winter. The railway line runs right up to the entrance. In 1944, some fifteen thousand Jews were arriving here daily. Enough. There are just no words, but the whole experience sears itself into my memory.

As our coach departs this bleak and misty scene for the long journey to Wroclaw, there is a palpable silence among the group. We are re-gathering our thoughts. In my mind a poem of sorts is forming. I will put it on paper later tonight in the comfort of my hotel room in Wroclaw. This darkness will take time to dispel.

> I do not want to be here
> But I am.

I try not to remember
but I must.
I want to leave this place
and I can
With my head full of
Cascades of hair,
Mountains of suitcases,
And spectacles and shoes
And children's shoes …

They did not want to be here
But they were.
They tried not to remember
but they did.
They wanted to leave this place
but they failed
Leaving only
Cascades of hair,
Mountains of suitcases
And spectacles and shoes,
And children's shoes …

George Cunningham
on Monaincha, County Tipperary

George Cunningham is a teacher, writer and historian who has spent a lifetime recording and promoting the heritage and history of his native town, Roscrea, County Tipperary. There are many historic sites in the town, but when asked to choose a place that spoke to him, he opted for a hidden monastic site a few miles outside the town – Monaincha, the Bog Island.

We are travelling just a few miles out from the town of Roscrea, County Tipperary, just off the Dublin–Limerick road – the old Slí Dála, one of the great highways that radiated from Tara many years ago. A couple of hundred years ago we couldn't have travelled here because it was then a lake, Loch Cré, which was subsequently reclaimed. Fifteen hundred years ago, there was a holy island in the lake – Inis Locha Cré. It was one of a number of 'islands' in the lake, which was more of a bog really, so this island later became known as Móin na hInse – the Bog Island – hence Monaincha.

A couple of saints were associated with the hermitage – St Canice of Aghaboe – which is about ten miles to the northeast, across the Nore – and St Cronán of Roscrea. For both of these men, Monaincha became their Skellig Rock – their place of hermitage where they could pray and do penance. The two men were roughly contemporaries of the early Christian Church. Canice was the older man and there is certainly greater mention of Monaincha in his life story, but Cronán eventually won out in his claim to the island by sheer proximity. He was simply nearer to it than Canice but we know from accounts of their lives – written later in the twelfth century – that there was a certain rivalry between them over Monaincha. I would argue that Monaincha wasn't a separate monastic site, but was rather the hermitage site attached to Roscrea.

Over the years Monaincha became well known as a place of pilgrimage in the then-known world (around the twelfth century). In Munster it was even better known than Holy Cross Abbey. The four most famous places of pilgrimage in Ireland were Croagh Patrick in the west, St Patrick's Purgatory in the north, Glendalough in the east and Monaincha in the south. When the Norman chronicler, Gerald of Wales, came to Ireland, he recorded the story he heard that no one could die here and he called this place *Insula Viventium* – the Island of the Living or Inis na mBeo, as it became known. Gerald subsequently spoke about it on his lecture tours abroad, and Inis na mBeo was eventually recorded in the Book of Ballymote as the 'Thirty-First Wonder of the World'! Don't ask me what the other thirty wonders were, but simply relish the privilege of visiting the thirty-first wonder a thousand years later.

Of course Gerald got the story all wrong. It was a spiritual story that indicated that when your sins were forgiven, it was your soul that didn't die, but that didn't stop Gerald's literal telling from spreading all over Europe – so much so that at the end of the fifteenth century a German pilgrim, Ludolf von Munchhausen, came all the way to 'Lan Nimmeo' or Inis na mBeo. His diary survived and was published. Even earlier than that, in the tenth century, a famous character in Irish ecclesiastical and state history, Flaitheartach, sought refuge on the island from the Vikings who followed him here, but he survived and became the Abbot and King of Cashel. This is recorded in the Annals. Further on, in the seventeenth century, Pope Paul V, in an effort to bring devotion back to places of pilgrimage, granted a plenary indulgence to visitors to Inis na mBeo. So popular had it become that in 1611 the Lord Deputy complained that 'fifteen thousand people – and some say many more' gathered here on a Sunday in June to do the penitential rounds.

In 1974 we revived Monaincha as a place of pilgrimage when crowds walked out here from Roscrea – several thousand people. Mass was celebrated at the church door and I gave a homily on the spirit of the place:

> This holy site can lay claim to a very special niche in our history, both local and national. No great battles were fought here. No great political events occurred. It is rather the spirit created by this place which has earned its right to fame. This little Romanesque church beside me, built with patience, skill and love – the large stones transported across bog and lake – stands as a wonderful monument giving glory to God ... We could not pray for anything better here today than for peace.

Prior to 1974, the story of Monaincha had gone out of memory, mainly because of changing ownership of the surrounding land. The Birch family acquired it at one stage and have a townland named after them – Birchgrove – and they also had a famous distillery here. They denied all burials on the island and it became off limits for the general public.

We just passed over a little rise on the road that was in fact another island before the lake was drained, Lady's Island as it is known. From here we walk along the pathway under Norway spruce trees and there it is – Holy Island, framed by lovely beech trees, with its predominant feature, the beautiful Romanesque church. The late Harold Leask, when he was Inspector of National Monuments, said he thought that this was the most magnificent church ruin in Ireland 'for site completeness, interesting detail and overall appearance'. We are standing in front of the doorway and to our left is a High Cross that depicts the clothed figure of the crucified Christ on the upper part, very much weathered now. The church is a twelfth-century nave and chancel church with a west-facing doorway that has three heavily decorated arches. Above the doorway is a later fifteenth-century window. This, in a way, tells the story of little churches like this – their ups and downs. If money became available – through pilgrims' alms for example – improvements and embellishments were made.

After Cronán and Canice who had probably flimsy wooden churches, the culdees or *Céli Dé* (they were thought by some scholars to be spouses of God) came here around 800 AD. Their austere practices attracted pilgrims here.

They were a reforming breakaway movement who were tired of the easy life of the Church. Then major change came with the Europeanisation of the Celtic Church in the twelfth century. The Augustinian order came to Monaincha and Roscrea and it was they who probably built this stone church. They would have lived here as a small community, looking after the pilgrims. We have some wonderful medieval prints of Monaincha.

This is one of my favourite places in the world. I have been lucky to travel a lot in recent years with my wife, Carmel, but I still regard this as a very special place. In my childhood this was on the way to Birch's Bog, where I came every summer with my father to 'save' the turf. My earliest memory is of coming to the bog on the bar of my father's bike, passing by this site – of which I knew nothing at all. It was never spoken of in schools. It wasn't on my radar until I began to take an interest in my own locality and educate myself in its history. I began teaching in 1961 and did all the usual things – played golf, courted, joined the musical society – but there was always this niggling thought that life was going by and I knew nothing! In 1968 a school tour from Roscrea went to see the round tower at Ardmore and in the process passed our own round tower in Roscrea without even noticing it! I said this must be wrong and why doesn't someone do something about it. 'Why don't *you* do something?' was the reply. That was what triggered me into educating myself about my own environment, including Monaincha. It wasn't that it was unknown. It had been studied and written about, but that was for an academic elite. I wanted to make it known for everyone and I did! For the past fifty years I have been recording its story both in print and visually.

We are now in the roofless nave of the church, surrounded by the tombstones of the Birch family. It reminds me of a verse I read once, written by someone who knew they would never be buried inside a church. He directed that the following be inscribed on his tombstone –

> Here lie I at the chancel door
> Here be I because I am poor
> The farther in, the more you pay
> Here lie I as warm as day

This was quite a big church for its time. On the right of the nave are three windows, a very narrow original and two larger ones from the thirteenth century. The other major feature is the chancel arch, built of sandstone – a soft stone that masons loved as it was easy to work with. The masonry here is superb. These stone slabs would have been hauled across the lake, maybe in winter when the lake was frozen. This building is a sermon in stone, telling the story of Ireland in microcosm. In the sixteenth century there was quite a lot of land attached to this church, but that was eventually taken over. Monaincha was separated from Roscrea and became Corbally parish. Before that the dampness of the island had got to the monks and they left here for Sean Ross on the mainland. Towards the end of the eighteenth century the Birches became owners of this place. The sacristy to our left was probably built in the fifteenth century and had an upstairs where the monks lived. There is a lovely window seat remaining. One can picture the prior sitting there, looking out over the bog.

I come here often. One of the beauties of the place is that you rarely find anyone else here when you visit, as we have done today. I suppose in a sense we have successfully kept this place a secret. I find a great sense of peace here and a sense of privilege that I was able to learn its story and to tell that story to others. It doesn't matter what the season is. Carmel and I come out here every New Year's Eve. We light a candle, say a prayer and just absorb the spirit and the peace of the place. Its story is a hidden story, but it is one that is there to be learned and savoured by anyone who wants to learn it.

There are various traditions about the place, going back to Gerald of Wales' 'island of the living' story. Also on a window ledge in the nave there is a large knob of stone. It is known as the Bread of Roscrea. Tradition has it that when Cromwell came to sack the place he couldn't find the way to here. He knocked at the door of a house in Roscrea. The terrified occupant was baking a loaf of bread. When she gave the information to Cromwell's troops, she returned to her kitchen to find the loaf of bread had been turned into stone. It's a lovely story but of course there's no truth in it. The embossed stone is probably part of a Romanesque feature, but that's tradition for you. Another tradition is that when doing the penitential rounds you stand with your back to the cross and reach back to join your arms around it. That tradition is also found at other penitential sites like Glendalough.

Monaincha is now a national monument, well minded by the state. It is a haven of remembrance, a quiet place to visit and savour. Places like Clonmacnoise on the tourist trail are finding it difficult to cope with the numbers of visitors. We don't have that problem here, thankfully, but we do have our moments. In the year 2000, to celebrate the millennium, the Cistercian monks from Roscrea came here on an afternoon during a Roscrea Conference and they sang Vespers in the nave. It was such an unforgettable experience to hear the monks' chant echo from these hallowed walls. Another great moment was in the late eighties, when the late Archbishop George Simms led an ecumenical pilgrimage to the midlands of Ireland, along with Kallistos Ware, an Eastern Orthodox bishop, and Bishop Michael of the Anglican Church. There were about fifty people in the group and I was asked to lead them around various sites like Lorrha, Kinnity, Aghaboe. I brought them here one afternoon. We left the bus up the road and walked down the causeway. The group sang hymns as they walked. Within the ruined nave I suggested we say an Our Father for peace – a *Pater Noster* in the language of the universal Church, Latin. In the middle of this I felt a tug on my sleeve from Bishop Kallistos who whispered – 'George, Latin is the language of the *western* Church'. So in the interest of balance we had the *Pater Noster* in Greek also. A memorable day!

I am proud to be of Roscrea and Monaincha is part of Roscrea's story. I love bringing people here. It is such a wonderful reminder of the great Christian heritage we have and whose legacy we are entrusted to pass on to future generations. I could talk forever about this place, but equally this place is forever talking to me.

Drumacon

I had completed the text of this book in March 2016 when, as a writer for children, I received an invitation to visit Oram National School in County Monaghan. Oram? That little village is but a few miles from Drumacon, the townland among the 'wee hills' that was home to my father and previous Quinn generations and was for me the location of magical childhood days when we were brought on summer visits to the Quinn homestead. If ever a place spoke to me it was Drumacon. Here surely was an opportunity to recapture the memory of those magical days.

I love the 'wee hills' of Monaghan with an intensity I cannot explain. Those beautiful rolling drumlins enfold each other so intimately and, in doing so, enfold me in their contours also. I suppose it is because my roots are here. My father was born and reared in the townland of Drumacon. He was the eldest of seven children born to Charles and Catherine Quinn, who worked a small farm of fifty acres that nestled among those wee hills. He joined the newly established An Gárda Síochána in 1922 and was stationed for the last twenty years of his career in Ballivor, County Meath, where I was born and reared. He never lost the love of home and every summer during my childhood, he bundled the four of us children into the back of a Baby Ford (and later, Ford Prefect) and brought us on regular trips to the 'wee hills'. On one memorable trip, as the Baby Ford rounded a bend at Broomfield in County Monaghan, a door opened and my sister Mary tumbled out onto the grass verge. No damage done, but we teased Mary about it for many years subsequently.

It is now 2016, the fiftieth anniversary of my father's death, and I am presented with an opportunity to travel those childhood roads back to Drumacon. It must be thirty years since my last visit. Will I remember my way through the intricate network of roads that will lead to the Quinn farm? I say a silent prayer to my father, seeking guidance as I set off on the Castleblayney–Dundalk road. I am to a large extent driving blind, desperately trying to unlock the route from memory. A few miles out, I take a left turn. The signpost says Toome but that doesn't register with me. I recall memories of particular landmarks such as 'Paddy Larry's shop', but where are they? Nothing for it but stop and ask. I stop at a modern bungalow which has a car parked outside. A man opens the door.

'Would you happen to know Brian and Patricia Quinn of Drumacon?'
'I would surely!'

Success! A lot more than success. This house is or was 'Paddy Larry's Shop'! I am speaking to Paddy Larry's grandson – who invites me in to show me a photograph of the shop as was, neat and thatched, and to meet his mother May, Paddy Larry's daughter.

'Och, sure wasn't I in your house in Ballivor many years ago!'

This is truly remarkable. By pure chance (or maybe not …) I have stopped at the very landmark that stayed in my mind. May and I exchange memories before I resume my journey, secure in my route knowledge. Over the bridge (weren't there dancing flags nearby where roadside dances were held on summer nights?), left at the T-junction, first right, up the brae and next left. Now of course everything is rolling into place. There was a flaxpool at that corner. Drumacon is real. When I had enquired at the hotel in Castleblayney, no one knew of Drumacon, mainly because the staff were not from these parts. I wondered if I was seeking another Brigadoon – the mythical Scottish village that only appears every hundred years – but no, this was Drumacon. This was the road I walked in later years with my father. These were the fields that we roamed as children. This was home.

The house hasn't changed outwardly at all. Unusually, there is no front entrance. I must go down into the yard (or rather 'the street' as it is known) to announce my arrival. What I always loved was the cosiness of this place – how the house, stable, stores, barn and byres all enclosed 'the street'. Of course the modern farm features sizeable sheds and barns beyond, but the cosy rectangle hasn't changed at all. When Brian and Patricia recover from the surprise of my arrival, I am invited into the kitchen for tea and conversation. The kitchen. Still the focal point of the house. I could close my eyes and see the ghosts of my uncles and aunts seated around the fire, discussing the matters of the day in that lovely Monaghan idiom.

'I hear Podgy's mother is poorly.'
'Och I'm right sorry to hear that.'
'Podgy'll not manage at all if she goes ...'

There's Uncle Charlie, pleasant and jovial, a 'terror for the reading'. He will marry Kathleen and they will run the farm. There's John the saddler and Jemmy the farmworker, neither of whom will marry. Both of them gentle, soft-spoken, kind and caring, interested in us as children. There's Katie, wise and gentle and loving. A pot of porridge bubbles over the fire, which is kept strong by the turning of a bellows wheel. This intrigues us as children and we crave a turn at the wheel, to watch its effect on the fire. There are silences. The clock on the mantelpiece ticks. There is warmth and comfort here. The bowls are taken from the dresser and the adults have porridge for supper, while we children indulge in a real treat – a slice of bread, generously plastered with golden syrup.

I take a walk outside to relive further memories. The farmhouse is single storey but at one end there is an upper room – now a bedroom, but in my childhood a loft – Uncle John's loft, where he practised his arts in saddlery and cobbling. Access to the loft was by an external stone stairway. A visit to the loft was for me sheer bliss. Uncle John perched on a stool before his bench, cigarette in mouth, deftly tapped a rhythm on his last or wrestled with

a horse collar. Ranged along his bench was a collection
of strange and wonderful tools – hammers, knives, awls,
pincers, lasts, vices – and wafting through the air was the
unmistakeable scent of leather. John was ever welcoming
to me. I was never an intruder but a work companion. He
would select a special 'wee hammer' for me, offer me some
leather off-cuts and brads (tiny nails) and leave me to my
own make-believe world of cobbling. I loved being in his
company and when he died a relatively young man in 1955,
I grieved for him greatly. When I wrote my novel for adults,
Generations of the Moon, forty years after his death, he became
James McKevitt:

> The loft was transformed into a workshop. Hughie
> and Pete built a workbench which ran the length of
> the room. James wrote to his former employer in
> Dublin and, within a week, a large consignment of
> leather, waxen thread, nails and various tools arrived
> at the railway station in Culloville. James was a very
> meticulous worker and arranged the tools and materials
> of his trade neatly around the room. Sarah loved to
> visit the loft, if only to inhale the comforting smell of
> leather and to marvel at the array of tools that hung
> on pegs along the wall. As James gradually picked up
> work, the number of visitors to the house grew and
> brought added interest to the life of the McKevitts.
> Although the customers gained access to the loft by an
> external stone staircase at the gable end of the house,
> their comings and goings were acutely observed by all

of the family and were often the source of livelier than usual conversation over supper.

'Hasn't Barney McQuillan aged a terror!' Bridie would say. 'I didn't recognise him going up to the loft with the stoop that was on him.'

The stone stairway is gone, but that solid gable wall will forever seal a hoard of golden memories of pleasure-filled hours in Uncle John's loft. Gone too is the well – or rather filled in – redundant in these days of rural water schemes. The well was at the top of the lane, just across from the house gable. Its darkness, depth and mystery were an attraction for a curious child. I am at one with Seamus Heaney:

I loved the dark drop, the trapped sky, the smells
Of waterweed, fungus and dank moss.

('Personal Helicon')

Especially in summer, when the water level was low and I threw stones down into the dark and awaited the splash that would 'set the darkness echoing'. Often I was startled by enormous spiders scrambling up the well wall, disturbed by my soundings. The well was of course a source of danger for a child and we would be issued with regular safety warnings. Even more so in the case of the flaxpool that lay beyond the sheds, a relic of previous decades when flax was a valuable cash crop in this area. I have no memories of flax in the fields but Aunt Katie would paint the picture for me:

'Och, the blue of the flax, in flower. It would take your breath away. People going the road would stop to look at it …'

Later it would be pulled by hand and immersed in the pool for 'retting', which would soften the fibre. In my childhood the flax pool was a dark and dangerous place, to be avoided save for tossing stones in from a safe distance, and wondering what slimy creatures they might disturb. Nearby was an orchard whose fruits we tasted in season, however bitter. Further on was the haggard where two giant haystacks provided the goals for endless epic hurling games between my brother Noel and myself. Constant disputes. If the ball lodged in the hay, was it a goal or not?

I return to the street. The outhouses have hardly changed. There are the stables, where Jemmy kept his magnificent plough horses, the byre where the barrel-bellied cows with their swaying udders ambled up the lane to be milked. Other sheds housed a pig or two and a flock of garrulous hens. I have a memory of helping Aunt Katie find a maverick hen who was 'laying out' – another memory that found its way into my fiction:

'Chuck-chuck! Come on my wee lassie. I know you're laying out somewhere hereabout. We've been watching you for a week now – me and Saint Anthony – and you're not doing my old back any good with all this stooping. Chuck-chuck!' … She cut a gentle swathe through the nettles to reveal the Rhode Island Red squatting on a crude nest under the innermost part of the hedge. 'Aren't you the bold lassie causing me all this trouble!' Bridie poked the stick through the puffed-up feathers. The hen moved away reluctantly to reveal five eggs in the nest. 'God bless Saint Anthony! Never failed me yet!', Bridie panted as she sank painfully to her knees.

(*Generations of the Moon*)

Further up the street is the barn, which has a hay loft at one end. Another place of dust and shadow where a boy could explore, burrow and hide and dream and imagine. There might be fearsome giants and brave warriors ...

Across the road is the brae, a steep hill sweeping up to the sky. There was a time when we skipped and panted our way to the top, but today arthritic knees make it too daunting a challenge. No matter. The memory remains. The hedge at the top is literally the border between two states. On the other side is County Armagh. The same wee hills, but another state. The view from the top of the brae is majestic. If you look really hard you can see seven lakes. And then the descent. We children invented a game called 'roly-poly'. You simply lay down, stretched your body out and rolled all the way down to the bottom! It was exhilarating. How we did not inflict serious injuries on ourselves I do not know, but apart from an occasional scratch or a reprimand for grass-stained clothes, we survived each time.

I return to the house. More tea and conversation. Then Patricia produces the photograph. 'See how many you would know there!' she challenges. It is an astoundingly clear print of a photograph that is over a hundred years old. It features the children of Dromore National School, 1914, evidenced by the slate held by a girl in the front row. It is a quite extraordinary photograph. The children stare seriously at the camera. Not one of them is smiling. And each one of them is dressed in their Sunday finery – girls in their neat dresses, buttons and bows, boys in their smart jackets, broad collars and dicky bows.

'That big lad at the back might be a Quinn,' I say.

It is indeed Uncle John. The young lad whose farming days ended when a stone crushed his foot at the age of seven. His parents would later send him away to learn the trade of cobbling as an alternative way of life. This is as far as I get with recognition.

'Well that's Jemmy in the front row,' Patricia points out.

Jemmy! Looking like Little Lord Fauntleroy in a tweed suit, broad collar and dicky bow, squinting at the unfamiliar camera.

'And there at the other end of the row,' Patricia continues, 'is Susan.'

Susan. My aunt Susan. The ten-year-old girl with the wistful, quizzical look in her eyes, hands folded in her lap. Susan. In twenty years she will be dead, having married, been widowed, remarried, become pregnant and died from appendicitis when doctors refused to operate on her. Susan. The tragic Susan. I have never seen a photograph of her before – at any age. I am choked with emotion. I can't take my eyes off this photograph. The young cobbler, the young ploughboy and that shy young woman whose life would span a mere three decades – all of them innocent and bemused, probably hardly even aware that in Europe a great war was under way, as they posed for this photograph.

'You can take that with you,' Patricia tells me. 'We have copies.'

My cup overflows.

Soon I must take my leave. Down the lane, back down the brae, left and then right, over the bridge and past Paddy Larry's. Tomorrow I will visit Oram school and tell the children of my love for Drumacon and the magical farm nestling among those wee hills. And on my way home to Galway I will stop at the cemetery in Castleblayney and pay my respects at the graves of those gentle souls, who in their time led honest and simple lives and to whom I will be forever indebted for their nurture and their love.

Acknowledgements

Extract from 'Living in the Country' by Patrick Kavanagh on page 85 is reprinted from *Collected Poems*, edited by Antoinette Quinn (Allen Lane, 2004), by kind permission of the Trustees of the Estate of the late Katherine B. Kavanagh, through the Jonathan Williams Literary Agency.

Michael Coady quotations from *Two for a Woman, Three for a Man* (1980), *Oven Lane* (1987, 2014) and *All Souls* (1997) are reproduced by kind permission of the author and The Gallery Press, Loughcrew, Oldcastle, County Meath.

Extract from 'Ben Madigan' by Alice Milligan on page 44 is from *Hero Lays*, published by Maunsel & Co., 1908. Copyright © Alice Milligan.

Extract from 'The Islandmen' by Richard Rowley on page 47 is from *City Songs and Others*, published by Maunsel & Co., 1918; 1913. Copyright © Richard Rowley.

Extract from 'The Coasters' by John Hewitt on page 48 is from *John Hewitt Selected Poems*, published by Blackstaff Press, 2007. Copyright © John Hewitt.

Extracts from 'Personal Helicon' (page 230) and 'Death of a Naturalist' (page 18) by Seamus Heaney are from *Death of a Naturalist*, published by Faber & Faber Ltd, 1966. Copyright © Seamus Heaney.

Extract from 'In Gallarus Oratory' (page 125) by Seamus Heaney is from *Door into the Dark*, published by Faber & Faber Ltd, 1969. Copyright © Seamus Heaney.

Extracts from 'Squarings' – 'viii' (page 129) and 'xlvii' (page 127) – and 'The Schoolbag' (page 18) by Seamus Heaney are from *Seeing Things*, published by Faber & Faber Ltd, 1991. Copyright © Seamus Heaney.

Extract from 'Anahorish' (page 17) by Seamus Heaney is from *Wintering Out*, published by Faber & Faber Ltd, 1972. Copyright © Seamus Heaney.

Extract from 'Alphabets' (page 19) by Seamus Heaney is from *The Haw Lantern*, published by Faber & Faber Ltd, 1987. Copyright © Seamus Heaney.

Extract from 'Station Island' by Seamus Heaney entitled 'A Vision of Master Murphy on Lough Derg' (page 22) was read by Seamus Heaney on *Education Forum* on RTÉ in November 1979. A later version appears in *Station Island*, published by Faber & Faber Ltd, 1984. Copyright © Seamus Heaney.

Every effort has been made to contact the copyright holders of the material reproduced in *This Place Speaks to Me*. If any infringement of copyright has occurred, the owners of such copyright are requested to contact the publishers.